Public Funds, Private Provision

The last decade has seen welfare systems throughout the Western world challenged as governments launched major efforts to stabilize or reduce government social expenditures and to return a larger share of the responsibility for social welfare services to private hands. This fiscal crisis and its accompanying theme of retrenchment coincided with the emergence of neoconservatism that has led to polarized debate and a significant change in attitude and policy regarding the role and function of government in society.

Public Funds, Private Provision analyzes the respective roles of government and the voluntary sector in the financing and administration of social services. Focusing on developments in British Columbia from 1983 to 1991, when the Social Credit government actively pursued a policy of privatization, this book examines the growth of the voluntary sector there and presents data which track the impact of privatization on services. It examines the issues of funding and accountability of the voluntary sector as it adopts the public agent role and increasingly delivers services on behalf of government.

In its discussion of the new partnership between government and the voluntary sector, this thought-provoking book raises important issues about government privatization policies and about the possible effects these policies will have on the future of the welfare state in Western society.

Josephine Rekart is a research consultant working in areas of social policy and social research. She has had a long-term association with the Social Planning and Research Council of British Columbia (SPARC) and has worked with various levels of government and non-profit agencies. She has also taught at the School of Social Work at the University of British Columbia.

Josephine Rekart

Public Funds, Private Provision: The Role of the Voluntary Sector

UBCPress / Vancouver

ISBN 0-7748-0428-9 (hardcover)
ISSN 0-7748-0453-X (paperback)

Canadian Cataloguing in Publication Data

Rekart, Josephine
  Public funds, private provision

  Includes bibliographical references and index.
  ISBN 0-7748-0428-9 (bound). – ISBN 0-7748-0453-X (pbk.)

  1. Voluntarism – British Columbia. 2. Social service –
  Government policy – British Columbia. I. Title.

HN110.Z9V647 1993   361.6'15'097711   C93-091484-8

This book has been published with the help of a grant from National Welfare
Grants, Health and Welfare Canada, and from the Social Sciences Federation of
Canada, using funds provided by the Social Sciences and Humanities Research
Council of Canada.

UBC Press gratefully acknowledges the ongoing support from the Canada
Council, the Province of British Columbia Cultural Services Branch, and the
Department of Communications of the Government of Canada.

Set in Stone by Brenda and Neil West, Typographics West
Printed and bound in Canada by D.W. Friesen & Sons Ltd.
Copy-editor: Camilla Jenkins
Proofreader: Carolyn Bateman
Indexer: Joanne Richardson

UBC Press
University of British Columbia
6344 Memorial Road
Vancouver, BC V6T 1Z2
(604) 822-3259
Fax: (604) 822-6083

For Michael, Emma, and Edward

Contents

Figures and Tables

Appendix Tables

Preface

In reaction to the influence of neoconservatism and the unfavourable economic climate of the mid-1980s, the Social Credit government of British Columbia adopted policies designed to reduce government expenditure and to return the responsibility for social welfare to private hands. These developments have led to a sustained and mounting debate about the proper roles of and interrelationships between government and the voluntary, commercial, and informal sectors in the social services.

These roles and responsibilities have yet to be mapped out, and much of the debate over privatization and discussion about the evolving roles of government and the voluntary sector has been fundamentally ideological. There is little information available in Canada on provincial government policies with regard to privatization in the social services. It is not surprising that there is even less information comparing policies between provinces across Canada.

I have tried to redress this lacuna by providing some very basic data to help trace the role that is, or has been, played by the voluntary sector in the social services in British Columbia. This work examines the growth of the partnership between government and the voluntary sector and the accelerating trend in which third parties operate as public agents to carry out public purposes. The evolving role of the voluntary sector is discussed in the context of the restructuring of welfare by neoconservatives. Restructuring involves a changed role for the state, the encouragement of a pluralist supply of welfare services, and an increased reliance on other sectors, notably the voluntary and informal sectors.

This right-wing support is virtually indistinguishable from support from the left, which also advocates a larger role for the voluntary sector, and which has long argued the importance of pluralism, self-help, and mutual help in social service provision. Although quite different philosophies are behind the increasing support of the voluntary sector, the apparent overlap suggests that a return to greater reliance on the sector for social service delivery has wide political appeal. An important question therefore arises: Is such reliance on the voluntary sector a cost-cutting strategy or is it a means of decentralizing bureaucratized and centralized government services in order to create provision that is more responsive to local needs? Other issues related to the voluntary sector include the growth of different forms of provision and the implications for the for-profit sector, the nature and possible functions of government in relation to the other sectors, and the increasing support for the voluntary sector in light of both restrictions on social expenditure and government withdrawal from direct service delivery.

An integrating theme in the book is that government has always been a pervasive influence in the activities of the voluntary sector (even prior to developments in the mid-1980s), although the extent of that influence has not been emphasized. It has probably been in the interest of both government and the voluntary sector not to divulge the number of tax dollars received by the latter. The false impression has therefore been allowed to gain ground that government cutbacks would have little impact on social services because the voluntary sector can and does provide a vast array of services and programs anyway. Given the misleading conclusions that are drawn from this thesis, it is time to demystify what the voluntary sector can accomplish on its own.

The pilot project for this inquiry was undertaken in 1987. It examined the impact of the 1983 Social Credit government's restraint program on the voluntary sector in British Columbia. The pilot study showed that instead of decreases in funding, the agencies surveyed showed a dramatic increase in funding from purchase-of-service agreements with the provincial government. On the strength of that finding it was proposed that the current province-wide study be undertaken to track government funding of the voluntary sector, with the substantive thrust of the research focusing on privatization or contracting out.

The Social Credit government, in power since 1974, was defeated in the provincial election in the fall of 1991. This book therefore focuses on the era 1983-93 when the Social Credit government, following a neoconservative plan to deal with its fiscal crisis, pronounced privatization as an explicit objective of social policy. In 1992 the newly elected New Democratic Party appointed a Commission of Inquiry into the Public Service and the Public Sector, defined broadly to include those bodies created, financed, or maintained by the province for public purposes. The results of this inquiry, together with initiatives to regionalize health service and to move social services from a child-centred to a family-centred system, are likely to introduce far-reaching changes in the way non-profit organizations relate to government.

I am indebted to the Social Planning and Research Council of British Columbia (SPARC) for sponsoring the study on which this book is based and for providing the support and encouragement to carry it out. I am particularly grateful to the following members of the advisory committee: Andrew Armitage, Barbara Brett, Marilyn Callahan, Michael Clague, Glenn Drover, Michael Goldberg, Fern Jeffries, Bruce Levens, Jack Macdonald, Carol Matthews, Gerald Merner, and Andy Wachtel. They were unfailingly generous and patient with their time, reviewing each chapter and providing much-needed critical and constructive suggestions. Funding for this investigation, as well as for the pilot, was provided by Health and Welfare Canada, National Welfare Grants Division. Evariste Thériault, research consultant to the National Welfare Grants Program, has provided advice, suggestions, and support throughout.

The views expressed in this book are those of the author and do not necessarily reflect those of the Social Planning and Research Council of BC, the Advisory Committee to the project, or Health and Welfare Canada.

I could not have completed this work without the help and advice of all those individuals in the voluntary and governmental sectors who contributed their time to be interviewed. Simon Trevelyan's assistance in carrying out the numerous interviews and in coding the quantitative data is much appreciated. Responsibility for the use of the data and for any errors of fact or interpretation is of course mine. Calvin Lai, programmer analyst at the University Computing Centre, University of British Columbia, provided invaluable assistance and advice on programming and statistical analysis. I wish to thank Phaik Lim Tan, who typed the bibliography and the tables. Thanks are also due to Dr. Tirthankar Bose for editing an earlier version of this book. I also wish to acknowledge the encouragement and support I received from Jean Wilson, senior editor, and Holly Keller-Brohman, managing editor, at UBC Press. Camilla Jenkins did an excellent job in copy-editing the text.

Finally, I want to express my gratitude to my husband, Michael, whose life has been intertwined with this research. He has contributed to its accomplishment through his support, patience, and judicious advice.

Public Funds, Private Provision

Introduction

This inquiry examines the respective roles of government and the voluntary sector in the funding and delivery of social services, particularly in British Columbia. It also examines the implications for the voluntary sector as it assumes a major role in delivering services on behalf of government.

The 1980s saw a major assault on the set of governmental social protections that had come to be considered as a correlative of the modern welfare state. A search for economies in social spending began in the mid-1970s and became more urgent in the 1980s. Changes in the economic and political climate prompted a major restructuring of our economy and society. These factors have led to a revival of interest in nongovernmental alternatives to deliver social services and have also cast doubts on the principles from which the welfare state has evolved.

Although the welfare state has always been subject to critical appraisal, these criticisms were not taken seriously until the mid-1970s. The recession of the early 1980s gave renewed eminence to the New Right, or neoconservative, philosophy, which advocated returning social service functions to the supply and demand dynamics of the free market. The key element of this philosophy is the reduction of the size of government to make way for the private sector. Underpinning neoconservative ideology is the belief that private provision is more efficient than public provision because it encourages competition and gives the consumer greater choice. Public provision discourages private sector initiative, encourages dependency, and stifles personal initiative and responsibility. This ideology advocates a non-interventionist government philosophy that favours the market economy through competition and sees the price mechanism as the engine of economic growth.

During the 1980s, governments everywhere launched major efforts to stabilize or reduce government social expenditure and to return more responsibility for social welfare services to private hands. The introduction of market factors as indicators to evaluate efficiency in social service provision has been widely described as 'the privatization of welfare.' This marked a radical shift in philosophy away from collective and toward private provision of social services. The social welfare policy debate in the 1990s reflects an underlying assumption that government can only partially support the provision of welfare services. This has been accompanied by a greater interest in the role of the market in welfare services.

Social policies in British Columbia have always allowed for a mixed economy, in which welfare services are available from both public and private sources. The dramatic expansion of both federal and provincial governmental responsibility in social welfare in the 1950s and 1960s led most observers to conclude that government had undergone a gigantic enlargement at the expense of other social institutions, especially non-profit organizations.

Observers' focus on government expansion in social welfare also ignored the long-standing, elaborate network of collaboration between government and the voluntary sector in British Columbia. Indeed, by the 1980s the foundations had been laid for a new kind of collaboration. In the policy shift toward privatization of the social services, voluntary organizations became partners with government, delivering services on government's behalf under purchase-of-service agreements.

Although *Public Funds, Private Provision* focuses on the voluntary sector, it is recognized that this sector represents only one of four engaged in social service delivery in British Columbia. The other sectors are the government, the commercial, and the informal sectors. The informal sector, namely services provided by family and friends, remains the main source of care in spite of the growth of government. The commercial sector encompasses services paid for by individuals, and its role in the social services has been the subject of sustained debate. The informal and commercial sectors do not fall within the scope of the book, and nor does it attempt to propose a program for the development of either the voluntary sector or social services in general. Instead, it focuses on the relative roles that are played and have been played by government and the voluntary sector in the funding and delivery of social services.

Specifically, *Public Funds, Private Provision* examines the issues of funding and accountability of the non-profit sector as it adopts the public agent role and increasingly delivers services on behalf of government.

Finally, the book looks at how dependence on government funding is also pushing the sector toward greater integration into the private market economy, as voluntary organizations try to walk the tightrope between providing services for government and retaining their organizational autonomy.

The inquiry includes a survey of 133 non-profit agencies in twelve communities, representing small, medium, and large metropolitan communities in British Columbia. It focuses on ministry programs directed to families and children, but does not use a narrow, 'legalistic' definition of family and children's services. The methodology and scope of the project are described in Appendix 1. The basic data gathered in this research, from which the figures and tables in the text have been generated, are tabulated in Appendix 2.

Throughout the book the terms 'non-profit' and 'voluntary' are used interchangeably. They refer to the broad spectrum of agencies engaged in providing direct social services and operating in concert with the government sector. Some of these organizations are tax exempt and some are incorporated and registered provincially as non-profit agencies. The agencies may employ volunteers, paid workers, and paid professionals to do much of their work, and they are formally controlled by a volunteer board of directors. Their nature may be summed up as follows: 'The key elements of this ideal type are that a body should be a formal organization, constitutionally separate from government, self-governing, non-profit distributing (as opposed to non-profit making, as many voluntary bodies raise finance through trading nowadays) and of public benefit' (Brenton 1985:9). This definition excludes hospitals, universities, art and culture groups, museums, foster-care providers, and nursing homes. Fee-for-service arrangements with family physicians and other professionals are also excluded from the analysis.

Chapter 1 summarizes the literature and demonstrates that the search for economies in social spending and the ideological shift away from state collectivism have together given rise to support for a much larger role for the voluntary sector. There is much in common between the New Right's stance on minimal government and the position of welfare pluralists, who advocate replacing government with the voluntary sector for social service delivery. The two viewpoints are nonetheless distinct. While the New Right advocates minimal government in both funding and delivery of social services, welfare pluralists believe that government should function as the main financier and regulator of social services but that service delivery is less relevant to it.

Chapter 2 provides a historical overview of government-voluntary sector collaboration in British Columbia. The relationship is discussed in terms of two models: the parallel bars and the extension ladder. Developments in social welfare since the 1960s and 1970s laid the foundation for voluntary agencies to increasingly assume the public agent role. Through the contracting relationship, voluntary organizations are playing a much more integral role in social service delivery.

The more governments use voluntary organizations as public agents or as instruments of social policy, the more necessary it becomes to monitor the funding relationship between the two sectors. Chapter 3 examines aggregate expenditure patterns in the Ministry of Social Services. Given that governments everywhere have for some time attempted to stabilize and reduce social expenditure, it is important to establish whether contracting out of services within major program areas has led to a decline in government expenditure. This chapter also examines the various sources of funding, and notes the proportions derived from different sources for the 133 voluntary organizations surveyed.

The use of voluntary organizations as instruments of social policy also raises arguments in favour of public funding for these agencies. The increase in government funds funnelled into voluntary organizations has brought pressure for improvements in accountability. Chapter 4 examines the extent to which the notion of fiscal, process, and program accountability is applied to this sector. It also attempts to link accountability to effectiveness and responsibility. The chapter demonstrates that there is confusion over what the agencies should be held accountable for and how accountability can be secured.

Chapter 5 examines the ways in which government, through its control of funding, defines and shapes policies and practice within the voluntary sector. It also explores the strategies used by voluntary organizations to counteract and resist those pressures. Because of the strings attached to government funding, and the difficulties of fundraising, voluntary organizations are increasingly finding that they must provide services on a fee-for-service or self-financing basis in order to respond to their own constituents, or to client needs beyond the tight guidelines defined by government departments.

Chapter 6 summarizes the research behind *Public Funds, Private Provision* and discusses issues related to the future of the partnership between government and the voluntary sector.

1
New Thinking on the Voluntary Sector: The Emergence of a Public Sector Role

As Western nations searched for ways to cut back social spending in the mid-1970s and 1980s, they became increasingly interested in an expanded role for the voluntary sector in providing social services. Rapid economic growth during the postwar decades had allowed social programs to develop under the assumption that the welfare state should complement the market economy and mitigate against any inequalities generated by market forces. As growth gave way to stagnation in the 1970s and deep recession in the 1980s, however, the erosion of government revenue brought intense pressures on governments to curb spending in all sectors. This fiscal crisis and its accompanying theme of retrenchment coincided with the emergence of neoconservatism, polarizing debate over the role and function of government in society and prompting a significant shift in attitude and policy.

The oil crisis of 1973, the financing of the Vietnam War, the abandonment of the gold standard, and several other factors triggered and then intensified an economic crisis. Lower rates of economic growth and investment and high rates of unemployment ensued. By the late 1970s, growth in government was not being matched by an expansion of the economy. It was in this environment that Milton Friedman's doctrine of monetarism took root. His conservative critique insists that the welfare state, with its associated taxes, distorts the incentive structure and interferes with the operations of labour markets, thereby encouraging dependency and stifling entrepreneurship and growth. Walker (1982) argues that a shift in official attitudes toward public expenditure resulted from various factors: high inflation triggered by the oil crisis; the economic downturn that began in 1974 and gave way to recession in the 1980s; public resistance to increased taxation; and escalating public sector borrowing, which deepened the inflationary spiral. The economic crisis brought to a head 'the bias against the public sector and the predominance of economic values over social values ... [which] remained hidden while economic growth was sustained' (Walker 1982:11).

The Canadian Context

Like those of other western nations, Canada's social welfare system is under strain. Restraint, retrenchment, and a growing emphasis on the need to reduce government to make way for the private sector are important themes that have polarized debate over the welfare state. Unlike in Britain and the U.S., however, the politics of neoconservatism in Canada makes few ideological attacks on the welfare state and organized labour. Instead, a large and growing deficit and problems of revenue co-mingle with debate about federal-provincial arrangements and the future of the country itself. The demands of Quebec and the other provinces over regionalism, provincial rights, and greater decentralization of federalism are really about the appropriate division of responsibility between the federal and provincial governments, in terms of both jurisdiction and the costs of social programs.

Canada's social welfare system[1] emerged out of federal-provincial arrangements arrived at in the earlier part of this century, when the federal role became defined by its responsibility to fund, rather than to operate, programs. The British North America Act (BNA Act) gave the federal government 'all of what were then considered significant governmental roles together with the most important sources of taxation, leaving the provinces with what were perceived as relatively minor responsibilities and, correspondingly, with minor sources of tax revenue' (Guest 1987:6). Constitutional interpretation placed health and welfare under provincial jurisdiction, but the provinces lacked the revenue base to undertake these responsibilities.

The federal government came under increasing pressure once it became obvious that the response of provincial and municipal governments was inadequate to meet the scope of emerging welfare demands as Canada developed into an industrial economy in the 1930s and 1940s. A series of constitutional amendments between 1940 and 1960 created federal involvement in income security through the provincial surrender of some constitutional jurisdiction. Financial programs that are labelled income security and affect all Canadians – such as child benefits, unemployment insurance, and pensions – are now under federal jurisdiction. These programs demonstrate a decidedly high level of centralization when contrasted with health and social services, which are in theory, and increasingly in practice, the responsibility of the provincial governments (Banting 1987a). Provincial governments have the responsibility to operate social services but funding for them may be drawn from different levels of government, as well as from the private sector. The costs for some areas of social spending within the jurisdiction of provincial governments are shared with the federal government, for example social services under the Canada Assistance Plan. Similarly, social assistance and social services for the needy are under provincial jurisdiction, but the cost is divided between the provincial and federal governments.

In conceptualizing the idea of the welfare state, Esping-Andersen (1989) advises researchers to move away from looking at the battery of social programs and levels of social expenditure. He argues that this linear formulation cannot explain either the different types of welfare states or their prospects. He suggests that Titmuss's (1968) conceptual approach, which distinguishes between residual and institutional[2] welfare states, is much more useful because it forces researchers to look at the contents of the welfare state. Using social participation and distribution as his criteria, Esping-Andersen identifies three types of welfare regime:

(1) The social democratic regime, as developed in Scandinavia, in which 'all strata and classes are incorporated under one universal insurance system; yet benefits are graduated according to accustomed earnings' (Esping-Andersen 1989:26). There is universal solidarity behind the welfare state. By promoting an equality of the highest standard this regime effectively crowds out market forces.

(2) The corporatist regime,[3] as developed in continental Europe, in which benefits or rights are attached to class and status and preserve status differentials. There is a strong commitment to preserving traditional family values, and the state plays a residual role. In other words, entitlement to income security and publicly subsidized services are strongly influenced by sentiments emphasizing that the state will only intervene when the family is no longer capable of servicing its members. For example, eligibility for continued assistance once unemployment insurance is exhausted depends on the family's capacity to support its own. Family benefits and the underdevelopment of certain types of services encourages mothers and wives to stay at home.

(3) The liberal welfare state, 'in which means-tested assistance, modest universal transfers, or modest insurance plans predominate' (Esping-Andersen 1989:25). This model is heavily influenced by traditional, liberal, work-ethic norms, which means that entitlement rules are strict, benefits are modest, and a stigma may be attached. This type of welfare regime is typical of most Anglo-American democracies, including Canada.

In Esping-Andersen's (1989) critique of the class mobilization theory, he applies the class coalition thesis to explain the emergence of these different welfare state regimes. (Class mobilization theory deals with the growth of the working class and the level of trade unionization in influencing welfare state development.) Although the working class has increased its power in the postwar period, its influence in the political sphere has not depended on organizational capacity alone. The success of working-class parties has depended upon their ability to forge alliances with other classes. Esping-Andersen's argument is that the Keynesian welfare state grew out of the ability of strong working-class movements to enter into political alliances initially with farmers' organizations and, in the post-Second World War period, with the new middle class. In the earlier phases of industrialization this coalition between the working class and farmers' organizations was based on the working class winning certain rights in return for farm price subsidies. The rural classes formed the largest electorate and it was to this group that the working class looked for coalition building. After the Second World War, the decline in political significance of the rural classes and the rise of the new middle class meant that 'the challenge was to synthesize working class-white collar demands without sacrificing the commitment to solidarity' (Esping-Andersen 1989:29).

Except in Great Britain, where coalitions between the working class and the middle class were forged much earlier, the political position of the new middle class since the Second World War has played a central role in determining the different types of welfare regimes. Thus, the success of the Scandinavian social democratic model depended on working class-middle class solidarity. This was achieved by providing universal rights of the highest standards to all strata and classes (Esping-Andersen 1989:29). In the liberal welfare state regime, as in Canada, the welfare demands of the middle class are allowed to be met in the market, through private insurance and occupational fringe benefits. Given that the middle class constitutes the largest electorate, and given its success in meeting welfare needs privately, it is not surprising that further extensions of the welfare state, which would involve higher taxes, are resisted and dualism[4] is further encouraged.

> The risks of welfare state backlash depend not on spending, but on the class character of the welfare states. Middle class welfare states, be they social democratic (as in Scandinavia) or corporatist (as in Germany) forge middle class loyalties. In contrast, liberal residualist welfare states found in the U.S., Canada and, increasingly Britain, depend on the loyalties of the numerically weak, and often politically residual social stratum ... [T]he class coalitions in which the three welfare states were founded, explain not only their past evolution but also their future prospects (Esping-Andersen 1989:31).

Attempting to locate Canada within a broader analysis of general historical processes, Jenson (1989) asserts that the development of the welfare state in Canada was not organized or sustained by class-based collective identities. The working class in Canada has never occupied a privileged position in the policy bodies of the state or achieved the status of 'social partner.' The canal and railway building era in the nineteenth century saw the growth of the industrial working class in Canada, but the class failed to forge an alliance with the politically powerful farmers in central and western Canada. The failure to forge this alliance undermined their ability to exercise power in the political sphere (Wolfe 1989). Within these different labour groups, ethnic, regional, and sectoral differences undermined cohesiveness and political effectiveness. It was not until the formation of the Co-operative Commonwealth Federation party (CCF)[5] in the 1930s that these differences were overcome. Even then, divisions remained to weaken the effectiveness of the Canadian working class compared to its counterparts in European countries.

Both Jenson (1989) and Wolfe (1989) offer explanations for the particular type of Keynesianism[6] that evolved in Canada. Jenson (1989) notes that as the Canadian economy expanded dramatically after the Second World War, it took on certain unique aspects. These influenced the Keynesian policy that was adopted and thus provide the context for understanding the development of the welfare state in Canada. They were: (1) the importance of resource exports as a basis of economic development, (2) the pursuit of more open trade relations with the U.S., (3) the import of manufactured goods, and (4) the import of capital for resource extraction and processing. The last two have created staggering deficits in the balance of trade. These features of the Canadian economy led to a deepening cycle of interdependence with the U.S. economy. The solution to Canada's balance-of-trade deficit after the Second World War was 'a privileged access to the critical U.S. market' (Wolfe 1989:119) in the form of tariff reductions, and larger quotas of Canadian resource exports were allowed into the U.S. The threatened loss of privileged access, as the U.S. attempted to counter its own burgeoning trade deficit, led to the 1987 bilateral free trade agreement.

Jenson (1989) argues that Keynesian policies, designed to counteract the crisis of the Depression, could not overcome 'the profound structuring effects of a resource-based economy in which natural resources were distributed by geographic lottery' (Jenson 1989:80). Keynesianism had to be supplemented by regional development policies to deal with long-term structural unemployment. The repatriation of profits by multinationals investing in Canada's resource extraction and processing industries meant that jobs could not be guaranteed in local economies. The federal government had to intervene to ensure the flow of capital to the country to replace the profits flowing out. Federal intervention during the economic upswings of the 1950s and 1960s meant that the multinationals were never challenged to assume any of the social costs of development.[7]

Neoconservatives have suggested that this social spending has caused the large Canadian deficit, which increased dramatically in the 1970s. Brooks (1987) and McQuaig (1991) argue that the large Canadian debt can be attributed to increases in social spending as well as to reductions in personal and corporate taxes. Brooks argues that had Canada maintained taxation at 1974 levels the debt would have been roughly half of what it became by the early 1980s. McQuaig (1991) maintains that Canadian personal taxes are high only by U.S. standards but low compared to Germany, France, and Sweden (35.5 per cent of GDP compared to 38.1 per cent, 43.8 per cent, and 56.1 per cent in 1989 in these countries respectively).

Epp (1989) provides evidence showing that while the proportion of taxes paid by individuals in Canada increased from 12.2 per cent in 1946 to 22.7 per cent in 1986, corporate contributions have declined from 34.6 per cent in 1946 to 15.9 per cent in 1986. In 1946, Canadians earned a total of $5,827 million in labour income and paid $711 million in taxes (12.2 per cent). In 1986, they earned a total of $273,978 million in labour income and paid $62,136 million in taxes (22.7 per cent). In contrast, corporate profits for 1946 were estimated at $1,721 million, of which $654 million was paid in taxes (34.6 per cent). In 1986, profits totalled $86,168 million and $13,710 million was paid in taxes (15.9 per cent). Epp argues that instead of the refrain of public spending restraint that few Canadians even question, the government should be taxing corporations to shoulder their share of the burden.

Policies and programs to address these concerns of a resource-based economy after the Second World War grew out of a consensus, which saw a stronger federal government with a will to intervene as the solution to problems of the Canadian economy. This consensus expressed the need for a strong federal presence to provide guidance in a large and fragmented country: 'The social compromises and institutionalized relationships of the welfare state were rationalized in terms of the needs of the whole nation and of the federal system' (Jenson 1989:84). Thus, allegiance to federalism arose out of the economic needs of this large and loosely knit nation.

Economic crisis in the mid-1970s prompted a re-evaluation of the nation-building strategies and federal-provincial relations adopted under postwar conditions. Jenson (1989) maintains that cultural and regional disputes in Canadian politics are really about the way that federalism operates as a distributive system. Provincial governments question the fairness of distributional outcomes that place a burden on their provinces but favour central Canada. Collective identities based on regionalism, language, culture, and religion fuel the provincial governments' challenge to federalism and the idea of a single 'nation.' The 1960s debate around cultural dualism, disputes over regionalism in the 1970s, the abortive Meech Lake Accord in the 1980s, and the failed Charlottetown Accord in 1992 symbolize a re-ordering of the social and federal-provincial institutional relationships that had evolved after the Second World War. Jenson comments, 'Conflicts over the identity of the Canadian nation, the costs and benefits of continued association in a single economic unit, and the self-definition of the nation in cultural terms dominated the political agenda from the 60s ... Canadian politics from the late 60s until the Meech Lake Accord of 1987 was dominated by cultural and regional disputes which focused on the way that federalism operated as a distributive system' (Jenson 1989:85).

Rather than causing an out-and-out ideological attack, within the federal party system, on the welfare state and organized labour, economic hardship beginning in the mid-1970s led to a questioning of the postwar policies and institutionalized relationships on which the welfare state was based. As a result, the welfare state is being reshaped through changes to these policies and relationships. The system of political representation – based on class-oriented party systems – that characterizes much of Europe and Great Britain has never been the basis of organized party politics in Canada. Developments in social welfare, as in unemployment, pension, and health insurance, were supported by all three parties, which are rarely and only minimally distinguishable on ideological grounds. Myles (1988) and Jenson (1989) contend that all three parties are pragmatic and, above all, motivated by the desire to win and retain office.

The influence of neoconservatism in federal politics is evident in the implementation of the goods and services tax, the de-indexation of family allowances, more stringent eligibility rules for unemployment insurance, a freeze on federal spending on education and health care, and the extension of a 5 per cent cap on Canada Assistance Plan payments to the 'have' provinces of Ontario, Alberta, and British Columbia under Bill C-69.[8] As Jenson notes, however, 'the rationale for such neo-conservatism is carried by a discourse on regionalism, provincial rights and decentralization' (1989:89). At the federal level, Canada appears to have avoided the worst excesses of Reaganism and Thatcherism. Instead, the economic crisis seems to have opened up for questioning those very issues upon which the welfare state was founded: national identity and the proper role of federal-provincial relations. Debates over these issues have set the context in which the federal government has been able to whittle away at the welfare state without being noticed while the country's emotion focuses on the national identity.

The federal government's 1991 budget, which signalled that debt and deficit reduction were the major thrust of policy, represented a significant threat to the welfare state as we know it. Under this budget the 5 per cent cap on Canada Assistance Plan payments was extended for another three years through to 1994-5. Until the framing of Bill C-69, the costs for income assistance and social service programs initiated by the provinces were shared equally with the federal government, which contributed 50 per cent. Under the new rules, however, any increases in provincial government expenditure exceeding the federal government limit of 5 per cent will force the three 'have' provinces to shoulder a greater burden of the cost. It is not clear whether this 5 per cent limit on annual increases in federal transfer payments under the Canada Assistance Plan will be extended to the other provinces. The Canadian Council on Social Development has argued that the other provinces are likely to become reluctant to improve social benefits for fear that the same restraint will be imposed on them.

Another important development under Bill C-69 in the 1991 budget was the freeze in federal government payments on established program funding (EPF), which includes medicare and postsecondary education. The two-year freeze was extended for a further three years through to 1994-5.[9] In addition, the transfer of taxing powers to the provinces will see the diminution of the federal role and an increase in provincial government control in the collection and spending of taxes in these areas. Such developments are likely to have important consequences, especially for medicare, where the federal government has been able to use the threat of withholding transfer payments as a mechanism to ensure national standards. The diminution of the federal role raises some very important questions about how national standards will be maintained and enforced.

The 1987 Free Trade Agreement with the United States also carries important implications for social programs. Wolfe (1989) warns that while the excesses of Reaganism and Thatcherism may have been avoided in Canada, the 1987 bilateral trade agreement 'represents an attempt to introduce through the backdoor the excesses of neo-conservatism ... [T]he role of market forces will be greatly enhanced in determining the allocation of investment, employment and income, at the expense of state policies' (Wolfe 1989:120). As Canada's economy is drawn ever closer to that of the U.S., the need for competitiveness presents a challenge to Canada, with its generous social programs and its relatively social democratic outlook on the world. This attitude to government represents an important distinction between Canada and the U.S. To provide such generous social programs, however, governments in Canada have had to tax and borrow heavily. There is a growing sentiment that increasing competitiveness in Canada cannot be achieved without a diminished role for government.

The perceived need to downscale government's role in social services has become a shaping force in British Columbia's politics. Unlike the federal government and most other provincial governments, which did not relish an overt attack on the welfare state (Moscovitch 1986), the Social Credit government of British Columbia in 1983 endorsed that attack and provoked a major confrontation with labour and social movements opposed to its neoconservative agenda. The Social Credit government adopted the rhetoric of the New Right, slashed spending on social services and reduced the number of public service employees. It mounted a campaign to restrain social spending and reduce government involvement, advocating the reprivatization of social services to promote efficiency. In social services the provincial government moved to limit its direct service role to the statutory responsibilities of income assistance and child protection. The provision of other statutory and non-statutory social services was to become primarily the responsibility of the private sector, both non-profit and for-profit, and of the community at large. The Family Support and Community Development recommendations of the Community Panel[10] suggest that this narrow focus may change. However, it remains to be seen how new legislation will revise the mandate of the Ministry of Social Services to enable it to provide supportive services as well as services relating to protection of children. Olson (1993:1) argues that it will require a service delivery model 'that redefines the roles of MSS and contracted personnel and engages the community in ways that will enhance the support component.'

This policy stance has prompted a growing interest in the voluntary sector and its role in the delivery of social services. Changes in the economic and social climate and interest in nongovernmental alternatives to social service delivery have given rise to support for a much larger role for the voluntary sector. This has, in turn, led to re-evaluations of public sector funding of voluntary activity. These developments also raise questions about the interrelationship of the two sectors. The following literature review attempts to summarize the arguments in the current debate. While this chapter does not present a complete and exhaustive review of the literature, it attempts to draw from several fields to note representative positions, and demonstrates the growing support for the voluntary sector.

A Convergence of Ideology?

Since the mid-1970s, both right-wing and left-wing governments have agreed that the welfare state has been experiencing serious fiscal problems. While the two sides view public expenditure cuts from opposite ends of the ideological spectrum, they are virtually indistinguishable in their support for a much larger role for the voluntary sector. Nevertheless, the convergence stems from very different bases and need unravelling. Advocacy of a greater role for the voluntary sector has vastly different operational and practical implications for the opposing sides.

Until the mid-1970s, sustained economic growth had facilitated the expansion of the welfare state (Heclo and Wildavsky 1981), which had been 'the residual beneficiary of the Growth State' (Klein 1974:1). The downturn in the world economy from the mid-70s revived anti-collective philosophy, more popularly known as the New Right or 'neoconservatism.' Anti-collectivism had been dominant in the nineteenth century but had lapsed into obscurity. Its modern proponents include F.A. Hayek, Friedman, and the Fraser Institute in Vancouver, British Columbia.[11] The principles of the New Right are described by George and Wilding (1984) and Bosanquet (1983). While it is not possible to deal with all the different strands of this philosophy, it is important to trace the major elements in its increasing support for the voluntary sector.

Freedom, individualism, and a belief in inequality are the basic tenets of anti-collectivist thought. Individualism, or individual freedom, is closely interrelated with the functioning of the market economy, which is seen to operate in a beneficent way only if individuals are free and uncoerced, and 'a strong sense of individualism makes unnecessary or impossible large-scale state intervention or coercion' (George and Wilding 1984:21). According to George and Wilding's thesis, the basic principles of individualism are as follows:

(1) Many of the activities currently undertaken by government would be better undertaken by individuals.
(2) If individuals are freed from state interference and given proper incentives, economic development will follow.
(3) Many of the so-called 'social problems' said to be socially caused really arise from individual causes. Thus, the solution to these problems should be based on 'individual responsibility and individual choice' (Gamble 1979:150) rather than on government policy.
(4) Ascribing problems to social causes lessens the feeling of personal and individual responsibility, which is the basis of a responsible and healthy society – 'a society in which the vast majority of men and women are encouraged and helped to accept responsibility for themselves and their families ... who care for others and look first to themselves to care for themselves' (Thatcher 1977:81, 86).

Anti-collectivists also hold that the pursuit of egalitarian policies is incompatible with the notions of freedom and individualism. Friedman (1962) suggests that the pursuit of egalitarian policies in countries such as Great Britain explains why its efficiency and productivity between 1940 and 1980 lagged behind any other industrial society. The New Right's views have persuaded governments to adopt monetarist policies to curb inflation and to regenerate the economy.

The welfare state is said to create inefficiencies because wealth production is stifled by the parasitism of a large public sector which has 'crowded out' the private sector (Bacon and Eltis 1976). Public sector services are inefficient because they do not operate within the same constraints as private-sector services, making it difficult to drive them out of business or to take them over. The high levels of taxation required to pay for a large public sector further depresses incentives to produce wealth. In contrast, the market economy, through competition and the price mechanism, functions as the engine of economic growth in which 'the pursuit of selfish aims of the individual will normally lead him [or her] to serve the general interest' (Bosanquet 1983:17).

Embedded in the New Right's economic strategies to reduce public expenditure and taxation is an ideology concerning a minimal residualist role of government: 'The doctrine of the minimal state, one restricted to such functions as promoting the conditions for a market economy to prosper, as well as maintaining law and order and defence, but returning many other responsibilities to individuals and lower-order social institutions is also central to the philosophies of many thinkers on the right' (Brenton 1985:141). The welfare state is charged with failure to deliver the results that were expected from increased expenditure on social programs. It has, moreover, hindered the development of other sources of welfare, such as the family, the voluntary sector, and the market. These accusations, in addition to economic policies committed to curbing inflation, reducing public expenditure, and stimulating economic growth through strategies based on the monetarist philosophy of Friedman (1962), have led Gough (1979:12) to remark that 'it is difficult to avoid the conclusion that the welfare state is attacked by the new conservatism at least as much for ideological as for economic reasons.'

The Left's interpretation of these fiscal problems of government is quite different. Nevertheless, criticisms from the Left, too, have provoked a re-evaluation of the government's role in welfare provision. It views the fiscal problems of government as the result of its twin and conflicting functions in capitalist society (O'Connor 1973). Government assists in capital accumulation through expenditure on both the economic infrastructure and the social services. A fiscal gap results because government bears the costs while profits are privately appropriated. It is exacerbated by pressure for more and more government services and resistance to increased taxation.

Criticisms from the Left stem from an assessment of the achievements of the welfare state. Many social policy writers have shown that the welfare state has not delivered on what it promised and inequality persists in spite of increased social spending (Johnson 1987). Townsend and Davidson (1984) showed that in Great Britain there were considerable social class inequalities in health as measured by mortality. LeGrand (1982) showed that public expenditure on the social services in Great Britain favoured the higher socioeconomic groups (defined in terms of income and occupation). The Left charges that 'while the welfare state has undoubtedly brought about improvements in the standard of living of working people, it has failed to bring about any fundamental change in the socioeconomic structure and in the distribution of power and wealth' (Johnson 1987:43).

Left-wing critics view the persistence of inequality, in spite of increased social spending, as a manifestation of the contradictions of the capitalist state. The response to working-class needs has been minimal because the welfare state operates principally in the interest of capital. Offe (1984) argues that in the welfare state the less well-off have been offered material benefits in exchange for their support of a social order that favours the status quo. The welfare state is accused of being concerned with social control rather than social change. Johnson (1987) suggests that a review of Marxist critiques of the welfare state makes it difficult to defend it from attacks from the New Right, which are based on the same types of criticism. Although the two sides have different rationales, they both agree that the welfare state has failed to create greater equality in spite of increased social expenditure.

These assessments and practical judgments on the achievements of the welfare state are central to understanding the spread of support for a larger role for the voluntary sector 'even among those whose political sympathies have hitherto lain in the direction of state collectivism' (Brenton 1985:3). Such criticisms have led to 'a re-appraisal of the role of the state in social welfare' (Hadley and Hatch 1981:2).

The Voluntary Sector and Social Welfare

At the turn of this century the first resort in times of need was family and friends, the informal system of care. The private market was another avenue of help for those who could afford to purchase needed services. For the large majority, however, help beyond the informal system meant relying on some charitable agency, as public assistance was the exception rather than the rule (Guest 1986). Religion and social services were closely intertwined in the earlier part of this century, as voluntary and charitable organizations based on religious or ethnic loyalties proliferated in the absence of widely available public services. These organizations found it necessary even then to seek government funding to assist them in meeting pressing needs. Guest (1986) argues that the ad hoc nature of the activities of these organizations led to fragmentation of effort and fostered a crisis approach to services.

Voluntary agencies continued to play an important role throughout the 1950s and 1960s, when the federal and provincial governments expanded their responsibilities in social welfare. During this period citizen entitlement to basic social services as a right was for the most part established. A comprehensive system of social services was expected to replace the voluntary sector, which could be expected to wither away. Others felt that voluntary action would continue to be important but that it would change its function and nature and take on a greater vanguard role (Clague et al. 1984).

Voluntary organizations proliferated during the 1960s and 1970s in direct response to available federal and provincial government funding (Tucker 1984). The activities of voluntary associations signalled not only the deficiencies and gaps in government service provision but also the emergence of new social needs, such as those of the growing numbers of single parent families, the working poor, and other marginalized groups that remained outside the general prosperity. Grassroots and voluntary movements were also concerned with action and social change (Ng, Walker, and Mueller 1990; Clague et al. 1984). Throughout the period the role of the voluntary sector became increasingly defined in terms of its ability to identify new needs, to develop innovative programs and demonstration projects, and to assist people whose lifestyles did not conform to mainstream norms. Thus, the role of the voluntary sector is now frequently conceptualized as either complementary or supplementary to government provision. Where voluntary organizations provide services that are substantially different from government services they are seen as complementary. Where they provide additional services of the same sort as the government sector, they are said to supplement government provision. Some of these issues are further developed in Chapter 2.

Welfare Pluralism
Proponents of welfare pluralism envisage a change in the balance of responsibility and function between government and the voluntary, informal, and commercial sectors in welfare provision. Welfare plural-

ists advocate reducing government monopoly and increasing the role of the other sectors instead of concentrating responsibilities and functions in a monolithic public sector. In the abstract, the notion of welfare pluralism is fairly neutral with respect to the balance of provision among the four sectors. Yet interpretations of the term are far from neutral. Hatch and Mocroft, two prominent welfare pluralists, state, 'In one sense welfare pluralism can be used to convey the fact that health and social care may be obtained from four different sectors – the statutory, the voluntary, the commercial and the informal. More prescriptively, welfare pluralism implies a less dominant role for the state, seeing it as not the only possible instrument for the collective provision of social services' (1983:2).

Welfare pluralists point out that this approach is not to be confused with the New Right's call for disengagement or minimal government. They envisage a greatly improved and expanded voluntary sector but do not suggest that it should replace direct government provision. Increasing the role of the other sectors does not necessarily imply a corresponding contraction of the government sector. Johnson (1987), reporting on a European meeting to examine the relationship between established social services and new social initiatives, found similar sentiments expressed:

> Governments are encouraging and supporting new initiatives as part of policies of welfare pluralism. The new initiatives involved substantially more participation and a greater reliance on self-help, mutual aid, voluntary and informal help with social workers fulfilling a community rather than a casework role. It is significant that participants were in total agreement ... that the relationship between initiatives and established services is not one where the former will progressively substitute for the latter (Johnson 1987:56).

This call for a change in the balance of responsibility and function is accompanied by analysis of the strengths and weaknesses of the different sectors. Welfare pluralists view the state or government as a necessary participant in a pluralist system. They point to the superior ability of the governmental sector to provide universal and integrated planning, to set and monitor standards, to achieve equity and social justice through resource allocation, and to preserve democratic control. They argue that the service delivery role is less suited to government, however, because the public sector tends to be costly, large-scale, bureaucratic, inflexible, and resistant to innovation. The over-centralized and bureaucratic public sector is remote, impersonal, and insulated from popular control and public involvement. Although control and accountability are vested in the elected representatives, the professionalism and paternalism inherent in the public sector deter public involvement and it remains impervious to the grievances and preferences of those who are served. Leaving service delivery in the hands of the public sector perpetuates the view of the public as client and government as the provider.

The voluntary sector is perceived by pluralists to be an antidote to these ills. Voluntary organizations tend to be spontaneous, speedy, and innovative in their reactions to social problems. Because they are usually small they can respond to new problems flexibly and immediately. The voluntary sector also extends, complements, and provides alternatives to public sector social services, but it requires financial help from government if its role is to be expanded and extended. Financial assistance would help the sector to overcome its major weaknesses, which are related to 'diversity and specificity' (Wolfenden Committee 1978:58). Voluntary organizations lack statutory authority, are unevenly distributed, and tend to arise out of spontaneous need. Consequently, the sector is not likely to allocate its energies according to abstract criteria of need or equity. In other words, 'its resources are not deployed in a way that a beneficent deity or social planner, taking all factors into account, would wish' (Wolfenden Committee Report 1978:58). Shragge (1990), assessing the extent to which community-based structures in Montreal could play a central role in health and social services, argues,

> Until ASOs (Alternative Service Organizations) are available across the province, these organizations cannot claim to provide on a universal basis, and by default, government ... becomes the main provider. Although the ASOs provide an alternative to state provision in many communities, within the present structures only the State can provide on a universal basis, unless it is willing to establish structures that can bring social planning and the necessary resources to the local community so that social and health services can be planned and organized on an autonomous, decentralized basis (Shragge 1990:154).

Hatch (1980) proposes an analytic framework that views the role of the voluntary sector from two different perspectives. In the marginal model, the voluntary sector remains at the fringes of government-organized services, concentrating on minor problems and emergencies. This model tacitly assumes that increased government action is the answer to social problems. The integral model, however, gives the voluntary sector a more central role, and limits government involvement to that of financier and regulator of social services. Government moves away from direct provision and toward enabling other forms of provision to flourish. It provides the necessary finance to compensate for deficiencies and gaps in services and to stimulate and influence the development of the voluntary sector in a way that counteracts that sector's shortcomings. Assignment of the financing role to government is what distinguishes the welfare pluralist model from the minimalist residual model advocated by the New Right.

Gladstone (1979) advocates a 'radical welfare pluralism' model in which direct government service delivery is replaced by the voluntary sector. He sees greater collectivism as appropriate only for income maintenance. The role of service delivery is less fundamental to government and can therefore be left to voluntary action. He sees this occurring through a process called 'gradualist welfare pluralism,' which involves a gradual handover to the voluntary sector. Describing aspects of the model, Gladstone (1979) explains that it includes

> elements of decentralization (more local involvement in decision-making), de-standardisation (more support for innovative and experimental programmes) and de-professionalisation (more emphasis on informal caring and self-help together with a shift to prevention and the horizontal integration of services). In such a scenario the role of government gradually becomes the upholding of equity in resource allocation, the enforcement of minimum standards, the fostering of more pluralistic legislation and the use of fiscal and regulatory law for income maintenance and to reinforce a preventive approach (Gladstone 1979:101).

Johnson (1987) maintains that welfare pluralists usually begin their analysis with a litany of the shortcomings of state provision without recognizing that it was the failure of markets and voluntary action that led to state intervention in the first place. Although welfare pluralists recognize that pluralism implies provision from a variety of sources, they tend to focus more or less exclusively upon the role of voluntary organizations. They are more hesitant in their support for the commercial sector, which they claim needs regulating:

> A system of social services dominated by the commercial sector ... in important respects negates some of the objectives for which the social services are established. Hence ... criticisms levelled at the statutory services ... should not be taken as arguments for patterns of provision that are predominantly commercial. But there are likely to be situations in which commercial provision, when subject to safeguards to maintain the quality of service and when it does not have a detrimental effect on other sources of services, can contribute usefully to a plural system of services (Hadley and Hatch 1981:100).

As Johnson (1987) points out, however, it may be difficult to limit the commercial sector once pluralism takes hold. A greater role for the private sector may threaten the voluntary sector by diverting funds as well as taking over service areas.

Welfare pluralists and the New Right both criticize public sector services as ineffective, inefficient, and unresponsive. Welfare pluralists argue that government service delivery should be taken over by the voluntary sector. They also see the weaknesses of the voluntary sector as easy to remedy. In this view, government continues to hold together a framework within which pluralism can develop, and acts as financier and regulator. The government, as the only agency able to monitor standards and ensure an equitable distribution of resources, would counteract the limitations of the voluntary sector: its 'unevenness and unreliability, lack of correspondence to need, its specificity and its lack of coherence' (Brenton 1985:160). Eschewing the ideological principles of the New Right, welfare pluralists do not argue for either a reduction in government expenditure or a residual government role. Instead, they advocate a transfer of resources to community-based structures equivalent to what would have been spent in direct government provision.

Despite their ideological differences, both welfare pluralists and the New Right embrace the concepts of decentralization and citizen participation, though for quite different reasons. According to Walker (1984a), there are two strands to the New Right's philosophy of reducing government. One is that the large public sector is a costly tax burden and stifles individual initiative and responsibility. The other is that increasing competition by giving the private sector a larger role will lead to efficiency in the public sector. Walker (1984a) argues that the second strand is based on a 'least-cost' notion of efficiency rather than on improving the effectiveness of social services. He further argues that belief in market forces as the superior mechanism for allocating resources obscures the distinction between the goals of economic efficiency and of social equity. While economic efficiency is concerned with least cost, social equity is concerned with 'the impact of policy changes on the distribution of resources, status and power between different groups in society' (Walker 1984a:35).

Pluralism and Decentralization

The twin themes of decentralization and citizen participation pervade the writings of welfare pluralists. With their anti-bureaucratic and anti-professional implications, these themes partly account for the wide appeal of welfare pluralism. The arguments for decentralization follow from criticisms of the welfare state as being too centralized, too bureaucratic, and too authoritarian. Big government, which places power in the hands of bureaucrats and professionals, is seen as more intent on pursuing its own internal agenda than on responding to the needs and wishes of its electorate. In this view, the expansion of the welfare state contributes to the growth of big government and attracts the same sort of criticism. The public sector must be made less monolithic by decentralization, as understood by the political interpretation of Schumacher's (1973) 'small is beautiful' argument.

Decentralization means different things to different people. Smith (1985) and Shragge (1990) distinguish between administrative and political decentralization. Administrative decentralization refers to service delivery by local structures without the power to make decisions. Political decentralization implies that local structures are involved in decision-making and are accountable to the local community.

Pluralists tend to discuss decentralization in the context of participatory democracy: decentralization is considered a prerequisite for successful participation. Pluralists have borrowed heavily from Schumacher (1973) and Berger and Neuhaus (1977). The latter note that the current contradiction between wanting more government services and less government raises the question of how public policy 'is to address human needs without exacerbating the reasons for animus against the welfare state' (Berger and Neuhaus 1977:2). They argue that the large size and consequent dominance of government institutions lead to alienation and a loss of meaning and identity for individual existence. They propose that 'mediating structures are essential for a vital and democratic society' (1977:4) and that through these structures the public can once again become involved in service delivery and

policy-making. Thus, the pluralists' concept of decentralization empha-
sizes political decentralization and not simply moving service delivery
from central to local structures. The concept extends to partnership
with local people and local communities:

> Decentralization is limited to what can be done within government
> structures; we are concerned with the structures that stand *between*
> government and the individual. Nor, again, are we calling for a devolu-
> tion of government responsibilities that would be tantamount to dis-
> mantling the welfare state. We aim rather at rethinking the institu-
> tional means by which government exercises its responsibilities. The
> idea is not to revoke the New Deal but to pursue its vision in ways more
> compatible with democratic governance ... The paradigm of mediating
> structures aims at empowering poor people to do the things that the
> more affluent can already do, aims at spreading the power around a bit
> more – and to do so where it matters, in people's control over their own
> lives (Berger and Neuhaus 1977:7-8).

Pluralism is therefore one of the ways of promoting citizen involvement. By arguing that only in a decentralized system will people feel
able to participate, pluralism inevitably links itself to decentralization.
But pluralists also assume that participation in service delivery automatically leads to participation in decision-making. For instance, in
considering the contributions of the voluntary sector to pluralism, the
Wolfenden Committee equates voluntary action with participation and
participation with the diffusion of power. It is argued that voluntary
action is one of the channels through which disenfranchised consumers can effect change in society, 'as a means of enabling widespread
direct participation ... [T]hey will also be engaged in altering ...
[society's] nature both directly through the activities they undertake
and, less directly, through the signals sent by these activities to the
statutory system on the nature of shifts in public interest' (Wolfenden
Committee 1978:29).

Nevertheless, the idea that social services can be delivered from a
variety of sources cannot be equated with the diffusion of power. It can
mean that services are delivered by community-based structures without any decision-making powers. Political pluralism implies involving
consumers and service-providing agencies in decision-making. Hatch
and Mocroft (1983) distinguish between welfare pluralism (variety and
choice of social service provision) and political pluralism (participation

in decision-making). The presence of one does not guarantee the presence of the other. Shragge (1990) makes the same point, arguing that autonomous, decentralized service organization requires decentralized structures and a transfer of resources.

Pluralism and Privatization

Welfare pluralism occupies centre stage in the current literature because the quest to reduce public expenditure necessitates the development of nongovernmental sources of welfare. Johnson (1987) points out that there is something in welfare pluralism for all shades of the ideological spectrum. For the New Right, it presents a convenient formula for dealing with the problems of government overload. For the left, it promises what might be termed the empowerment of the people. It provides an opportunity for government to shift the responsibility for providing social services to the private market, thereby making way for the private, voluntary, and informal sectors.

There is a vast and growing literature on the topic of privatization. In the space available there is no possibility of attempting anything more ambitious than a brief synopsis of how the term is used.

Privatization is one of the strategies adopted by neoconservative governments as a way of rolling back the state. It has been used in several different contexts. LeGrand and Robinson (1984) contend that to understand privatization we must understand the way in which government intervenes in any social or economic activity. Government intervention may involve any or all of provision, subsidy, or regulation. It may provide a particular service or commodity through ownership of organizations that employ the relevant personnel. It may control the price of a commodity or service through subsidy by public funds, or provide the good or service free. It can also regulate provision through quality, quantity, and price regulations. Health care in Canada, for example, is made available through public provision of hospitals and government employment of the relevant personnel. Services are provided free at the point of use, and are regulated through qualification requirements. In the same way, government involvement can be described for education, housing, transportation, and other components that make up our system of social welfare. In each of these areas the extent of government provision, subsidy, and regulation varies.

It is not always easy to find the dividing line between the public sector and the private market in each component of the social welfare system. The picture is further complicated if one also examines the incorporation of private market practices into public sector services. Thus, although health care is provided free at the point of use, for example, health care in British Columbia is also financed by levying of insurance premiums. Given these difficulties it is not surprising that privatization in relation to the social services is a difficult concept to define:

> Privatization schemes differ not only in the type of state intervention whose reduction or elimination they require. They also differ in what is proposed in its stead. Some propose simply a replacement of the state by the market, [and that] the relevant service ... be undertaken by profit-maximizing entrepreneurs operating in a competitive unregulated environment. Other schemes involve the replacement of one form of state activity by another: a reduction in state provision, for example, coupled with an increase in regulation by private providers. And yet others want to encourage the activities of organizations that are neither the conventional profit-maximizing firms nor the state enterprise: charities and other non-profit making organizations, workers' co-operatives, consumer co-operatives, [and] community organizations (LeGrand and Robinson 1984:3-4).

Privatization therefore refers to strategies designed to reduce government provision, subsidy, and/or regulation. The mechanisms to shift responsibility from government to the private sector include:

(a) A general expansion of commercial provision and the closure of government facilities.
(b) The sale of [national] assets.
(c) Contracting out either entire services, or parts of a service.
(d) A reduction in public funding through cost-sharing charges or reduced subsidies.
(e) Fiscal and other measures designed to promote private provision.
(f) The use of more stringent eligibility criteria for the receipt of statutory benefits or services.
(g) Deregulation: freeing markets from government intervention and supervision (Johnson 1987:140).

Kamerman and Kahn (1989), summarizing the presentations of a number of authors, point out that the case for privatization usually begins with the efficiency-economy-choice argument. Those making this argument usually point out that non-profit and for-profit agencies are more cost effective, provide more choice, are more responsive and flexible in meeting social needs, and offer more scope for innovation and specialization compared to the public sector. Kamerman and Kahn (1989) point out that the evidence for this argument is, however, inconclusive. They assert that the differences between the sectors with respect to all these factors are modest and likely to be as great within sectors as across sectors, with size and area of service being important variables.

Authors opposed to privatization usually base their reservations on government motives. Because a mixed economy represents the status quo in most welfare states, it can be argued that by enabling governments to shift the public-private mix toward the private, privatization represents an attack on the state system of protection and social provision that has evolved to date. Encouraging 'mediating structures' is merely a screen behind which governments can decrease their funding on a scale that makes replacement impossible. Without being able to operate in some areas, and without public provision against which other types of provision can be measured, government is at the mercy of contract agencies and is unable to enforce standards and expectations.

These authors conclude that strategies to select policy areas in which the private sector can play a greater role are in essence about redefining the social role of government. Policy strategies cannot be debated without confronting the ideological issues that have to do with one's view of the role of government in society. Starr (1989) points out that in the current political context, privatization should be recognized as an ideological attack on societal responsibility. Titmuss (1968) and, more recently, Walker (1984a) suggest that the question for society is whether social costs that fall most heavily on the weakest groups in society should be underwritten collectively or individually or be allowed to 'lie where they fall.' Proponents of privatization may argue that the welfare state reality is really a blending of public and private leading to a 'mixed economy of welfare.' The danger is that those on the radical right would agree, and they have used this same argument to call for the downsizing of government, seeing minimal government as appropriate for promoting the conditions for a market economy to prosper and maintaining law and order.

Within the context of this book, privatization in the social services implies greater reliance on the voluntary, informal, and commercial sectors in financing and delivering social services. It refers to the adoption of market criteria – or the profit motive – to ration and deliver services. The effect is to restructure the balance between the public and the private in both financing and delivery. According to Walker,

> in the social services, privatisation (or privatism) more often takes the form of a partial inroad into the public sector. This may consist of the takeover by private enterprise of specific ancillary services, such as school meals or laundry services; more common is the introduction of charges or a self-financing criterion. In this context then, privatisation represents the introduction or further extension of market principles, in the public social services ... Privatization may be said to take place when responsibility for a service, or a particular aspect of service delivery passes, wholly or in part, to the private sector and when market criteria, such as profit or ability to pay, are used to ration or distribute benefits or services (1984a:25).

Thus, privatization in the social services is defined in a much broader sense than in other contexts, and does not have to be totally privately controlled or administered.

Between 1980 and 1986, the provincial government of British Columbia sought to reduce the size of its role in the provision of social services. This initiative, as will be outlined in the next chapter, was due both to the financial constraints occasioned by an economic recession and to a declared belief that government had become too large and pervasive. Within the Ministry of Social Services, the provincial government moved to limit its direct service role to the statutory responsibilities of income assistance and child protection. The provision of statutory and related services was to become primarily the responsibility of the private sector, both non-profit and for-profit, as well as of the community at large.

Summary

This chapter summarizes the arguments that have led to a growing interest in the voluntary sector and its role in the delivery of social services. The apparent overlap between the right and the left suggests that a return to a greater reliance on the voluntary sector has wide political appeal. The restructuring of welfare by neoconservatives is concerned with a changed role for the state and an increased reliance on other sectors, namely the voluntary and informal sectors. The voluntary sector has also received increasing support from state collectivists, who view private voluntary agencies as important mediating structures that can bring about decentralized and more responsive services to people.

In Canada and within the federal party system, the economic crisis of the mid-1970s did not lead to an ideological attack on the welfare state and organized labour. Instead, the postwar policies and institutionalized relationships on which the welfare state was based have been re-evaluated. Debates over national identity and the proper balance of federal-provincial relations have established a context in which the federal government has been able to whittle away at the welfare state without being noticed, while the electorate focuses its emotion on the national identity of Canada.

2
An Overview of Voluntary Sector-Government Collaboration in British Columbia

Despite the long and complicated history of collaboration over social services between the voluntary sector and government in British Columbia, researchers and policy analysts have paid little attention to it. Documentation of the collaboration is scanty, and must be gleaned from work that describes the development of the social welfare system in Canada in general and British Columbia in particular. It is only since the BC provincial government moved to reduce government through privatization under the restraint program it adopted in 1983 that questions about government-voluntary sector relations have been recognized as important.

Government Policy and Economic Change in British Columbia, 1980-6

In 1983, the Social Credit government of W.R. Bennett won its third term in office. This was seen as the electorate's confirmation of support for government restraint policies begun in 1982. While promising not to turn its back on 'those in need in our society' the Social Credit Government, in July 1983, launched its budget of restraint.

In this budget the government argued that restraint was necessary in view of the falling tax revenues resulting from the recession and the growing provincial deficit. Government revenues from natural resources fell from $1,319 million in 1979-80 to $544 million in 1982-3. Revenues from income and sales tax also declined in the same period (Callahan and McNiven 1988). In his budget speech, the Minister of Finance argued that government had grown too large and that the new budget was designed to pursue a 'leaner and more efficient government' (BC Ministry of Finance 1983a). It reduced full-time staff in direct government employment from 47,000 in the fiscal year 1983-4 to

40,000 in 1984-5, with further reductions planned for future years. In 1992 this figure was estimated to be 39,058 (Korbin Report 1993). Sales tax was increased from 6 to 7 per cent. A freeze was imposed on social assistance payments, while the numbers on welfare increased from 66,277 cases in 1981 to 146,021 in 1984 (Scofield 1984).[1]

The Minister of Finance also indicated that 'where possible government ... [intended] to give the private sector the opportunity to take over functions and activities not appropriate to government' (BC Ministry of Finance 1983a). Less government and lower expenditures were to be achieved through privatization.

Savings were realized through government downsizing and the elimination of a wide range of services. In social services the following were eliminated: the Community Involvement Program,[2] family support workers, the child abuse teams, and a transition house for battered women. The following were also abolished: the Employment Standards Board in the Ministry of Labour, the Rental Office in the Ministry of Consumer and Corporate Affairs, the Human Rights Commission, the Planning Branch in the Ministry of Municipal Affairs, and the Regional Resource Management Committee.

In addition, the government introduced twenty-three bills that, among other things, extended compulsory review of wage levels of organized workers and expanded management rights in the workplace. Widespread unrest followed the introduction of these measures. Opposition groups formed an alliance under labour-led Operation Solidarity, and organized a series of protest marches. A province-wide strike was averted following an agreement between the premier and the leader of Operation Solidarity, in which the coalition agreed to end 'the escalating job action in exchange for an unspecified government commitment to reconsider some elements of its July package' (Howlett and Brownsey 1988:142).

In 1984, the Social Credit government introduced a much more restrictive budget. Revenue was to be increased by 8.7 per cent through an 8 per cent surcharge on provincial personal income tax. Total expenditure was to be reduced by 5.1 per cent below the 1983-4 level (BC Ministry of Finance 1984a). The budget again emphasized reduction of government to make way for the private sector: 'The policy of reducing the size and scope of government will continue ... Regulatory processes are being streamlined and automated, both to reduce costs and ease the burden of compliance on the private sector ... [A] key element of the expenditure plan is the shifting of emphasis from the government to the private and non-profit sectors' (BC Ministry of Finance 1984a:9-10).

In 1984, the number of full-time equivalents (FTEs) in direct government employment was reduced a further 12 per cent. Between 1982-3 and 1986-7 there was a 26.5 per cent reduction in FTEs in the public sector (BC Ministry of Finance 1982b, 1983b, 1984b, 1985b; BC Ministry of Finance and Corporate Relations 1986b, 1987b). This caused an outcry because unemployment in the province was already at an all-time high. Schworm (1984) and Gideon and Schworm (1984) have argued that this downsizing contributed further to the pool of unemployed.

Many researchers have interpreted the Social Credit government's policies within the context of the rising importance of neoconservative ideology worldwide. Howlett and Brownsey (1988) argue, however, that attempts to place these developments within the international political, economic, and ideological environment ignore the importance of provincial political and ideological sensibilities. These authors demonstrate that the policies of 1983 and 1984 represented not a break with the past but a continuation of long-term strategies designed to protect the interests of large national and international companies on which the provincial economy continues to be dependent. The policies also ensured continued electoral support for the ruling Social Credit party.

According to Marchak (1984), British Columbia has always acted as a resource hinterland, first to Great Britain, then to the U.S., and now to both the U.S. and Japan. British Columbia differs from other resource-based economies in its extreme dependence on the export of raw materials from forestry and mining, which have formed the province's economic base. Another important point is that, since the Second World War, these resources have been increasingly exploited by large national and international companies which are under no obligation to use any of the wealth generated to invest in local secondary or manufacturing industries. Although the resource extraction activities created employment in the resource-rich regions, they did not allow the provincial economy to become more developed and self-sufficient. Expansion of employment in the forestry and mining extraction and processing industries, however, created a large working class located in the private sector.

The provincial government played a crucial role in encouraging the mostly American-owned companies active in the capital-intensive forestry and mining industries. The establishment and growth of these large-scale extraction and processing industries required that the provincial government provide not only a favourable investment climate but also the necessary communication infrastructure in transportation and energy development. As the provincial government became more involved in the economy after 1941, its activities created an expanded public sector made up of civil servants and a large working class dependent on such activities.

This postwar economic restructuring meant that the economic bases of small business and the traditional middle class moved away from resource extraction and toward 'contracting, speculation and services associated with government promoted transportation, energy and social service expenditures' (Howlett and Brownsey 1988:144). Significantly, a large proportion of the province's population therefore depends on state activities or expenditures for their livelihood. By the early 1970s,

> both the traditional middle class and small capital in the province ... owed their existence to contracting and services provided for the state and a resource sector now completely dominated by large domestic and foreign capital. The new middle class and the public sector working class were directly dependent on public sector spending while small capital and the traditional middle class were dependent on public sector spending and ancillary private sector expenditures (Howlett and Brownsey 1988:144).

The development of the different classes and their dependence on government expenditures (which underpinned their shifting alliances) is essential to understanding the basis of party politics in British Columbia. The alliances among the various classes can be interpreted within the context of an electoral conflict between the interests of labour and those of business. Thus, for example, faced with increasing labour militancy and a loss of support in the 1941 elections, the ruling Liberals formed an alliance with the Conservatives to keep the labour-controlled Co-operative Commonwealth Federation party (CCF) out of government. The alliance represented electoral support based on a coalition between small business and the domestic and foreign-owned companies. It fragmented as government policies became increasingly directed to the benefit of the large companies, and in 1952 the Social Credit party formed the government.

Social Credit was to remain in power until 1972. Its electoral support was derived from a coalition between big business, small business, and the traditional middle class, held together by their dependence on government expenditures on transportation and energy infrastructure development. Government spending further expanded public sector employment, as workers had to be hired to build and administer such development. The labour force in the province doubled and as the population in the province increased, a new middle class became associated with the public sector. It was employed in schools, hospitals, and other social services created to serve the needs of the growing population. The government began to attack public sector growth, however, as this growth began to constrain its ability to spend money on programs advantageous to the business sector.

Government attempts to reduce spending in the public sector threatened not only the direct employment of the new middle class and working class but also small business and the traditional middle class, dependent for their livelihood on continued increases in public sector spending. Government economic policies favouring the large domestic and foreign-owned companies had reduced the role of the latter two groups in the resource industries. Together with the middle class and the working class in the public sector, they formed an alliance with the working class in the private sector to defeat the Social Credit party in 1972.

During its short stay in power from 1972 to 1975, the New Democratic Party (NDP) antagonized its electoral support in the public and private sectors by introducing back-to-work legislation just prior to the 1975 election. According to Howlett and Brownsey (1988), the NDP also alienated the different groups representing business through its attempts to control profits. These various business interests formed a coalition under the Social Credit party to defeat the NDP in 1975.

The willingness of different business groups to unite under a Social Credit party ready to promote their interests through the vehicle of public expenditures is a recurrent phenomenon in BC provincial party politics (Howlett and Brownsey 1988), but the traditional middle class played a much more important role in the second coalition. They were now located in the rapidly expanded service sector and dependent on government expenditures. The increasingly significant part played by domestic and foreign-owned companies in the provincial economy diminished the position of small business in this coalition.

The declining importance of small business in the alliance presented a problem to the Social Credit government. It had to contend with the increasing electoral significance of the growing numbers of workers in the unionized public sector who supported the interests of labour. Continued public sector expansion again hindered the government's ability to promote the interests of those business groups upon whose electoral support it depended. Faced with the electoral power of the middle and working classes employed in the public sector and supporting labour, the Social Credit government in 1983 adopted policies designed to reduce the size of the public sector while promoting the interests of business. Thus, Howlett and Brownsey argue, the policies adopted in 1983 and 1984 were 'consistent with ... [the government's] long term aims of ensuring the continued operation of a provincial economy dominated by large capital, with its short term aim of ensuring that this promotion of large capital would not jeopardize the electoral support of small capital and the traditional middle class located in the private sector of the economy' (1988:164).

    In 1983, however, the government's intentions were far from clear. Its rhetoric on downsizing and privatization created much confusion and controversy for the social services, sparking ideological debates and raising the spectre of corporate and for-profit firms making inroads into domains that many considered to be the jurisdiction of government. Many and varied strategies were simultaneously implemented (Callahan and McNiven 1988; Rekart 1988), contributing to this confusion. Government action included the following:

    (1) The size of government was reduced by eliminating provision of non-statutory services such as family support workers, child abuse teams, family service coordinators, and services to street adolescents. It was questionable whether programs that continued to be funded could pick up the pieces since their budgets remained the same, or were decreased.

    (2) Provincial government funding through the Community Grants Program was decreased. The program funded voluntary and private agencies in order to provide preventative and developmental services. Macdonald (1984), in his survey of voluntary agencies in Vancouver, found that programs relating to women and children were especially hard hit.

    (3) The government also moved to reduce its responsibility within some statutory services through 'bureaucratic disentitlement[3] ... which is sometimes ... difficult to monitor because the exclusions are mandated through modifications in internal policy while leaving the legislative framework intact' (Callahan and McNiven 1988:20).

(4) Direct government service provision was consolidated and limited to the purely statutory services of child protection, income security, and adoption. New and existing statutory and non-statutory services were contracted out to non-profit and proprietary agencies and individuals. Where these services had been provided directly by government (as in twenty-two children-in-care resources in the Lower Mainland), they were now contracted out to former employees and private organizations. Outside the Lower Mainland, these services had always been contracted out. New services in juvenile justice and for the mentally handicapped were also contracted out. The trends in services for handicapped people toward deinstitutionalization and community living have resulted in residents of institutions being relocated to community-based facilities that are contracted out to non-profit and proprietary agencies.

(5) There have been some fundamental shifts in responsibility from the provincial government to other levels of government. In the field of child welfare, for example, the provincial ministry has developed a policy of transfer so that aboriginal people can assume control over their own child welfare portfolio. The federal government assumes responsibility for funding. This measure, although applying only to status Indians, involves a considerable reduction in provincial government responsibility, given that 35 per cent of children in care are native people. Similarly, in education, local school boards and municipal governments must raise taxes to make up for any shortfall in school operating budgets. Certain policy areas, such as spousal assault and family maintenance, have been redefined in order to limit the provincial government's responsibilities.

(6) Callahan and McNiven also maintain that although fee-for-service does not appear to be significant in family and children's services, user fees have increased for child day care. The reason is that government subsidies to low income families have declined in recent years, and so voluntary and proprietary agencies have had to charge higher fee levels to make up the shortfall between subsidies and operating costs. Those families who cannot afford this difference probably do not use child care services, suggesting that government may be subsidizing those who are better off.

Models of Voluntary Sector-Government Collaboration
The importance of the voluntary sector in the history of social service development in British Columbia has generally been eclipsed by a focus on federal and provincial government activity. The history of this sector

also shows the uneasy influence of the residual and institutional phi-losophies on social welfare. The voluntary sector role evolved in tan-dem with developments in federal and provincial responsibility in social services.

The relationship between government and the voluntary sector until the 1950s and 1960s can best be described in terms of two models proposed by Sidney and Beatrice Webb (1912), which have been called the parallel bars and extension ladder theories. The Webbs attempted to define a legitimate sphere for the voluntary sector that would be compatible with the greater responsibility assumed by the state in social welfare in Great Britain at the turn of the century. The parallel bars model describes a situation in which voluntary organizations provide services parallel to those of government, but for a different clientele. In the extension ladder model, voluntary agencies provide services 'that are placed firmly on the foundation of an enforced minimum standard of life and carrying out the work of public authorities to far finer shades of physical, moral and spiritual perfection' (Webb and Webb 1912:252). Implicit in the extension ladder model is the assumption that voluntary agencies do not have statutory powers and cannot undertake the responsibility of governments to provide universal services. Voluntary organizations merely add something extra to the framework of services provided by government.

Kramer (1981) calls attention to another feature of the relationship between voluntary agencies and government, which he presents as the public agent model. In this model, government makes contracts with non-profit and profit-making agencies to deliver services on its behalf through purchase-of-service arrangements. A preliminary study (Rekart 1988) undertaken to examine the impact of restraint on voluntary agencies in British Columbia showed that privatization in the province has involved an expansion of contracting out between government and private agencies, particularly voluntary agencies, for the delivery of social services. Through these purchase-of-service agreements, the government's role in service delivery has been reduced, and third parties – such as voluntary organizations – have acquired an important role in service delivery. Such third party arrangements involving voluntary agencies, private agencies, and self-employed individuals under contract either to agencies or to the government represent a clear alternative to government provision of social services. The following sections trace the history of the relationship between government and the voluntary sector in terms of these models.

Government Social Services and a Mixed Economy of Welfare in British Columbia

Prior to 1900, and under the British North America Act of 1867, social welfare[4] was seen by the federal government to be the responsibility of the provinces which, in turn, assumed it to be largely a local or municipal responsibility. Local government was to be a last resort for the dependent or 'worthy' poor, and to discourage the 'unworthy,' financial assistance had to be below the minimum that a worker might otherwise be earning. The needy were not eligible for relief if they had relatives capable of providing for them. Only if the normal avenues of work and family were closed would individuals be allowed to receive municipal or local government help. When they were not eligible, or where such help did not exist, their needs were met by churches and private charities. Thus, the relationship between government and the voluntary sector during this early period conformed to the parallel bars model. Voluntary organizations with a religious base provided services parallel to those of government but for a different clientele.

From 1900 to 1927, the government of British Columbia passed a series of acts that provided the beginnings of a social minimum (Clague et al. 1984). The philosophy behind a social minimum is that 'there is a certain minimum of conditions without which health, decency, happiness and "a chance in life" are impossible' (Marsh 1950:37). The unavoidable poverty caused by disease and rapid social and industrial changes in a frontier territory challenged the idea that Canada was a land of opportunity. The increasing numbers of the poor also defied the notion that the amount of unavoidable poverty was negligible and did not require government action.

The YWCA, YMCA, Salvation Army, and Victorian Order of Nurses had already been established in Vancouver prior to the turn of the century. In 1901, the Children's Aid Society (CAS) was incorporated in response to the Infants Act of 1900, under which orphaned and neglected children became wards of the state. The CAS and the Catholic Children's Aid Society (CCAS) together received public funding to provide care for these children. During this early phase, during which the provincial government passed legislation to effect its own greater involvement in social welfare, private and religious charities played a major role in providing services and meeting the needs of the indigent. Local governments provided relief as a last resort to the 'worthy' poor. Despite increasing involvement, both the federal and provincial governments continued to see health and social service provision as the responsibility of local governments and private charities. The provincial government provided funding to private charities but did not itself assume responsibility for service delivery. Clague et al. (1984:6) found that 'in the first years of the 1900s, the Provincial budget expended about $100,000 annually on public charities.' These charities included mutual benefit societies, charitable institutions, and benevolent societies. The evidence suggests that the major input into welfare services in the nineteenth century came initially from private and religious charities, with the government filling in the gaps.

It appears that although these societies received public funding they also depended largely on charitable and volunteer effort. The extent of public subsidy to voluntary agencies was an issue even then. The Children's Aid Society found that it did not have enough resources to meet the demand, and campaigned vociferously for government to accept greater financial responsibility for child welfare and 'public responsibility for caring for wards' (Clague et al. 1984:6). Activism on the part of the CAS culminated in the reorganization of the society in 1927, after which point it received the bulk of its funding from the provincial government to provide statutory child welfare services. The lines between government and the CAS and the CCAS were already becoming blurred with this reorganization.

The Great Depression of the 1930s and its aftermath brought dramatic changes to the federal and provincial governments' role in social welfare. The response of the federal government to high unemployment across the country marked the beginnings of its responsibility for financial programs that affect all Canadians, such as unemployment insurance. Tables 2.1 and 2.2 summarize the major initiatives by the federal government of Canada and the provincial government in British Columbia in the fields of health and social services between 1927 and 1990. With the exception of social services for aboriginal people, veterans, and old age pensioners, financial programs that affect all Canadians are under federal jurisdiction. The provincial government is responsible for services that affect its residents, but financing for these services may be shared with the federal government.

From the 1930s on, responsibility for social welfare was also beginning to shift from the municipal to the provincial government, which had greater resources. The BC provincial government established the child welfare division in 1935 (later named the social welfare division), which eventually assumed responsibility for children's services in the rural areas. Branches of the CAS had been set up in rural areas but they

Table 2.1

Federal government initiatives in health and social services, 1867-1992

Year	Initiative	Description
1867	BNA Act	Provinces responsible for legislation relating to the social welfare of their residents.
1908	Annuities Act	Precursor of the Old Age Pension Act.
1927	Old Age Pension Act	Means-tested old age pension for persons aged 70+.
1930	Unemployment Relief	Means-tested emergency relief to municipalities to relieve destitution during the depression.
1937	Welfare Institutions Licensing Act	Ended the operation of commercial maternity homes and adoption services.
	Amendment to the Old Age Pension Act	Amended to cover blind persons.
1940	Unemployment Insurance	Contributory and universal insurance protection against unemployment for major sections of the labour force.
1944	National Housing Act	Federal grants for low-cost housing.
1945	Family Allowance Act	Universal children's allowance payments program.
1951	Old Age Pension Act	Replaced the Old Age Pension Act of 1927. Established a universal pension for all Canadians aged 70+. Repealed in 1966 and made universal for persons aged 65+.
	Old Age Assistance Act	New cost-shared program providing income supplement for people aged 65-69 who passed a means test.
1966	Medical Care Act	Protected all Canadians against major health care costs.
	Canada-Quebec Pension Plan	Employment contribution pension plan.
	Guaranteed Income Supplement	Covered all those at or near retirement but not covered by Canada Pension.
	Canada Assistance Plan	Consolidated all federal, provincial financial assistance programs that employed needs or means-test into a 'single comprehensive programme of benefits that would meet financial need regardless of cause.' Broadened the interpretation of need to include the working poor and expanded the range of cost-share services. Included for the first time federal cost-sharing with the provinces for child protection and child welfare services.

Year	Act	Description
1971	Unemployment Insurance Act	Unemployment insurance extended to cover all the labour force.
1984	Family Allowance Amended	Indexation limited to the amount of inflation that exceeds 3 per cent.
1989		Family allowance and old age security pension clawed back for those of higher income, ending universality of family allowance and old age security pension.
1990	Unemployment Insurance Act	Eligibility rules and federal government's financial involvement changed. Qualifying period increased and maximum duration of benefit reduced. Full cost shifted to employers and employees.
1991	Bill C-69	Cost-shared programs in Ontario, Alberta, and BC capped at 5 per cent until 1995. Two-year freeze on federal government payments to health and postsecondary education extended for a further 3 years. Transfer of taxing powers facilitating a diminution of the federal role.
1992	Child Benefits Act	Three programs consolidated into the Child Tax Benefit. Maximum benefits paid to families with net incomes up to $25,921. Reductions in benefits above this income threshold. Cut-off point established. Partial indexation. Earned income supplement component made available to families with earned income above $3,750 eligible. Maximum supplement of $500 for families with earned income between $10,000 and $20,921.
1993	Unemployment Insurance Act Amendment	Earnings-replacement reduced from 60 to 57 per cent of insurable earnings. Benefits denied to workers who quit without just cause.

Source: Clague et al., *Reforming Human Services* (Vancouver: UBC Press 1984); Myles, J., Decline or Impasse? The Current State of the Welfare State, *Studies in Political Economy* 26 (Summer) 1988:73-107; Canadian Council on Social Development, *Canada's Social Programs in Trouble* (Ottawa: The Council 1990); Caledonian Institute of Social Policy, *Child Benefit Primer: A Response to the Government Proposal* (Ottawa: The Institute 1992); Battle, K. and S. Torjman, *Federal Social Programs: Setting the Record Straight* (Ottawa: Caledon Institute 1993)

Table 2.2

BC provincial government initiatives in health and social services, 1867-1991

1900	Municipalities Act	Established duty of every city and municipality to make suitable provision for the poor and destitute.
		Destitute and Sick Fund founded.
		Public school system established.
1901	Infants Act Protection of Children Act	Provided for legal transfer of guardianship of orphaned or neglected children to the state.
1917	Workers' Compensation Act	Guaranteed workers compensation for injuries incurred in the course of employment in an employer contribution scheme.
1920	Mother's Pension Act	Provided a small monthly income for mothers with children under 16.
1927	Old Age Pension Enabling Act	Enabling act to take advantage of Ottawa's new Old Age Pension Act, a cost-shared program between the federal and provincial governments. Eligibility broadened to a less stringent means test.
1929	Male Minimum Wage Act	Established a minimum wage for male workers in the province; followed by female minimum wage act in the 1930s.
1935	Amendment to the Mother's Pension Act	Amendment to the 1920 Mother's Pension Act to include fathers who were totally incapacitated.
1937	Mother's Allowance Act	Replaced Mother's Pension Act.
1945	Social Assistance Act	Families without means no longer dependent on relief handouts from municipal governments or private charities. Broke new ground by including health services, occupational training and re-training, foster and boarding home care. Provided social assistance irrespective of race, creed, citizenship, or political affiliation.

Year	Act	Description
1948		Amalgamation of social welfare services.
		Provincial government reimbursed municipalities 80 per cent of costs for all social aid.
		Municipalities with over 100,000 people required to set up their own welfare departments or to purchase provincial service with funds provided through a per capita grant from the provincial government.
1958		New cost-sharing formula established between provincial government and municipalities to equalize welfare costs on a per capita basis throughout the province.
		Department of Social Welfare and Department of Health Services and Hospital Insurance established.
1963	Family and Children's Court Act	Established family court committees in large cities and municipalities to advise judges, and to act as resources for children before the court.
1974	Community Resource Board Act	Established the Vancouver Resource Board (VRB).
		Integrated statutory and non-statutory services under elected resource boards.
		Enabled resource boards to identify needs, establish priorities, monitor and evaluate services, and allocate community grants funding to community-based agencies.
1976	Gain Act	Replaced Social Assistance Act of 1945.
		Social services to be available to at-risk families and children.
	Family and Child Service Act	Revised 1901 Protection of Children Act.
		Updated 1963 Family and Children's Court Act but made no reference to provision of preventative services to families and children.
1977	Community Resources Board (CRB) Amendment Act	Eliminated CRBs and the VRB.
		Ministry of Human Resources assumed all child protection services across the province.
		Municipalities discharged from all responsibility for social services.

(continued on next page)

Table 2.2 (continued).

1978	Family Relations Act	Dealt with child custody, access, guardianship, matrimonial property, maintenance and support obligations in marriage dissolutions.
1980	Family and Child Services Act	Children in need of protection defined in terms of abuse, neglect, and living conditions that endanger their safety and well-being. Defines responsibility of superintendent regarding apprehensions.
1984	Young Offenders Act	Defined conditions under which a young person is subject to the same court procedure as an adult. Specified dispositions on convictions. Children under 12 may not be charged with contravening a provincial statute.
1985	Family Compensation Act	Permitted an action to be brought on behalf of a deceased's common-law spouse, and on behalf of a child of a deceased's common-law spouse if the deceased had supported the spouse's child.
	Family Relations Act	Empowered the courts to implement and enforce maintenance, custody, access, and guardianship orders.
1987	Adoption Amendment Act	Established a passive adoption reunion registry.
	Family Maintenance Enforcement Act	Designated a director of maintenance enforcement. Consolidated, streamlined, and established new remedies to expedite the enforcement of maintenance orders. Permitted the Crown to obtain and to make maintenance agreements for persons receiving GAIN.
	GAIN Amendment Act	Permitted filing of maintenance agreements or orders with the director under the Family Maintenance Enforcement Act for monitoring and enforcement under the act. Permitted the Crown to obtain reimbursement for financial assistance given when a maintenance order or agreement is in arrears.

Year	Act	Description
1988	Victim Rights and Services Act	Set out rights of victims. Imposed on the attorney general the duty of promoting and maintaining victim assistance services with money appropriated for this purpose, together with a victim fine surcharge.
	Family Relations Amendment Act	Empowered the court to decide who is the parent of a child where parentage is denied by a putative parent in a maintenance proceeding.
	Bill M204	An act to feed hungry school children.
1989	School Act	Learner-focused act which sets out entitlements and responsibilities of parents, teachers, school principals, school board officials, school boards, and the Ministry of Education. Home school recognized.
	Family and Child Services Amendment Act	Required the superintendent to provide the parents of a child with particulars if the child is apprehended.
	Adoption Act	Empowered the minister to provide financial and other assistance to adopting and adoptive parents. Empowered the superintendent of Family and Child Services to disclose, in certain circumstances, information relating to adoption of a child.
	Rights of Children in Care Act	Established rights of children-in-care. Established position of child advocate for the province at the Office of the Ombudsman.
1990	An Act for Better Child Care	To make available affordable, accessible, accountable, and responsive quality child care to all BC children aged 0-12 years in need of some form of non-parental supplementary child care.
	Family and Child Services Amendment Act	Required the superintendent to provide the parents of a child with a copy of the report to court and particulars if the child is apprehended.
	Adoption Amendment Act	Roles of parents, private adoption agencies, and superintendent of Family and Child Services defined in the adoption process. Simplified step-parent adoptions and revoking of consent for birth parents. Established licensing and regulation of private adoption agencies.

Source: Information to 1977 adapted from Clague et al., *Reforming Human Services* (Vancouver: UBC Press 1984); British Columbia, Legislative Assembly, *Bills* (Victoria: Queen's Printer 1978-91).

were not able to meet their obligations satisfactorily. The CAS and the CCAS continued to assume responsibility for children's services in the Lower Mainland and in Victoria. By establishing its own department of social welfare, the province developed and consolidated its responsibility for curative and preventative services to families. This move demonstrated that the development of direct government service provision was being given financial priority.

It is clear, however, that these government initiatives, in addition to services provided by existing charities and societies, could not meet the extra demands being placed on services. Expansion of government responsibility was accompanied by the emergence of other societies such as the Family Services Society of Greater Vancouver, the Family Welfare Bureau, and the predecessors of the United Way. Yet apart from monies for the CAS and the CCAS, the extent of government funding of the voluntary sector during this period is not known. Both societies were receiving the bulk of their funding from government and providing services to children under statutory authority. The relationship between government and the other voluntary agencies continued to be based on the parallel bars model.

The assumption that social services should be a public responsibility influenced the development of social welfare both during and after the Second World War. Brenton (1985:123) states that after the war, development was affected by the 'pure doctrine of social welfare.' This principle spurns the idea that social distribution should be based on 'charity.' The extension of federal and provincial responsibility in social welfare during prosperous postwar times fostered a sense of societal responsibility for meeting social needs. From the Second World War to the late 1970s, public perception of the welfare state was coloured by the principle that the public sector should expand, making nongovernmental alternatives redundant. In reality, however, the development of public sector responsibility for social services lagged behind these fine ideals.

As the provincial government broadened its involvement in social services during this period, there was some concern in the voluntary sector that the public sector would take over its functions (Clague et al. 1984). Throughout the period, government services developed alongside those provided by the voluntary sector. Callahan and McNiven (1988) suggest that some competition arose between the two sectors because many social work graduates preferred employment with non-profit agencies, which were perceived as providing better quality services. The non-profit agencies were also innovative in their approach to service delivery, and took part in advocacy. Uneven distribution of these agencies between rural and urban areas – many more were located in urban settings – contributed to the different perceptions of the two sectors. Rural areas had to depend on self-help or government for services. Urban areas, on the other hand, supported the development of a wide range of voluntary organizations employing professionally trained social workers. This promoted high quality service.

During the 1950s and 1960s, services administered and funded by government and those funded and administered by private and voluntary charities became clearly separate. It appears that as the federal and provincial governments became more deeply involved in welfare provision, the parallel bars relationship between government and the voluntary sector gradually developed into the extension ladder model. Voluntary agencies were providing services that extended government provision 'to far finer shades of physical, moral and spiritual perfection' (Webb and Webb 1912:252). Callahan and McNiven (1988:15) found that the two sectors 'remained separate from one another in planning, funding and delivery and often relationships were strained.' The separation was clearly marked by different spheres of activity. Voluntary agencies concentrated on preventative and recreational services, at the time considered to be on the fringes of government services:

> Governments either administered directly or closely regulated services to recipients of social assistance, child welfare services, probation services and services to persons in prisons, hospitals and psychiatric institutions. These services, many of which had a social control function, came to be known as statutory services in the sense that there existed a public statutory mandate for their provision. The voluntary sector at the time administered and funded group and recreational services of neighbourhood houses, casework services of [the] Family Services Association, and other traditional counselling services provided by non-profit agencies and church organizations (Macdonald 1984:2).

While voluntary agencies increased in number during the 1950s and 1960s, they do not seem to have ventured into new roles or new directions. Although their mandate no longer included health and income maintenance, voluntary agencies were slow to respond to new challenges. Instead, professional social workers expressed 'frustration with the multiplicity of agencies and confusing, overlapping jurisdictions' (Clague et al. 1984:19). Lack of funding was probably a major constraint to voluntary sector expansion into new spheres. There is no documentation of the scope of governmental financial support, if any, to voluntary agencies at the time, with the exception of the CAS and CCAS. In the populated metropolitan areas, voluntary organizations continued to play an important role because direct government social services were slow to develop. In addition, the demand for services was such that even with government sector expansion, reliance on the voluntary sector was undoubtedly necessary to meet the growing demand.

The mid-1960s ushered in a new phase for the voluntary sector and saw the growth of a closer relationship between it and government. In 1966, the Canada Assistance Plan was passed, legitimizing a broadened concept of social services. Cost sharing between provincial and federal governments was extended to cover

> those in financial need, as well as ... a broad range of personal and community social services ... [E]legible services were those having as their object the lessening, removal or prevention of the causes and effects of poverty, child neglect or dependence on public assistance, and included such services as rehabilitation programs for the disabled, casework counselling, assessment and referral, community development, consultation, research and development, homemaking services and daycare (Dunn 1980b:18-19).

The Seebohm Report (1968) from the U.K.,[5] the CELDIC Report (1970) from Canada (Commission on Emotional and Learning Disorders in Children),[6] Quebec's Castonguay-Nepveu Report (1976),[7] and Canada's Hastings Report (1972)[8] showed that fragmentation of services and lack of coherence were the major problems facing the organization of social services. The importance of an integrated approach to services was emphasized in all these reports. During the 1960s, a movement to include citizen participation in the planning, implementation, and evaluation of policies and programs also developed. This was, in part, encouraged by the Canada Assistance Plan, which provided federal funding for 'activities and programmes which foster the participation of consumers of welfare services' (Guest 1986:159).

In spite of the millions spent on social welfare by the federal and provincial governments, the gap between rich and poor refused to close. The welfare state was not meeting the expectations of equity and resource redistribution that it had raised. Different types of self-help groups and social movements came to life, partly due to the frustrations associated with the public welfare system and partly to advocate for changes in public policy. Voluntary organizations that arose during this period were somewhat different from the ones established earlier, which had been founded primarily to provide service. The new organizations were concerned with self-help, grassroots action, and social change, functions that brought about a 'broadening and radicalizing of the voluntary sector into community action and organization, protest movements and campaigns' (Brenton 1985:36).

The expansion of the voluntary sector received a great boost from federal job creation programs in the early 1970s. Through Opportunities for Youth (OFY) and the Local Initiatives Program (LIP), millions of dollars were funnelled into community services projects throughout British Columbia. At the same time, grassroots movements aimed not only at improving social services but also at bringing about social change mushroomed in the province. Advice and information centres were set up to help people find their way around the welfare state. Self-help and mutual aid groups attested to gaps in service provision.

In the early 1970s, the New Democratic Party (NDP) government of British Columbia passed the Community Resources Board Act, which was to change the collaborative relationship between government and the voluntary sector dramatically. The act was intended to create a system of locally elected boards for the social services, similar to hospital or school boards. It was a novel, radical, and controversial idea at the time to elect elements of the boards, because the political implications were never articulated. Some saw the structure of the boards as instrumental in creating local accountability for social services, while others believed that it had the potential to undermine the legitimate powers of the provincial government (Clague et al. 1984). The Community Resources Boards (CRBs) were established to integrate social services, decentralize decision-making, and encourage citizen participation in social service planning and delivery, thereby breaking up the monopoly on service delivery held by government departments and 'established' voluntary agencies. In Vancouver, the CAS, the CCAS, and the City of Vancouver Department of Welfare and Rehabilitation were taken over by government and amalgamated under the Vancouver Resources Board (VRB). The VRB was composed of a majority representation from fourteen locally elected CRBs.

The main responsibility of the CRBs was to decide how to allocate monies made available through the Community Grants Program. Global funding for social services was to be provided to these locally elected boards, which would then allocate it to non-profit organizations to deliver preventative and remedial services considered important at the local level. The Community Resources Board Act gave the CRBs the following responsibilities:

> to provide public participation in the planning and provision of social services and to encourage and support citizen involvement in all concerns that affect the quality of life in the community; to encourage an integrated service system and a preventive approach, to identify needs and establish priorities; to monitor and evaluate; to receive, administer and allocate funds from public and other sources in an equitable, rational manner (Clague et al. 1984:40-41).

In non-metropolitan areas the locally elected CRBs concentrated on preventative services through the grants mechanism. It was intended that the statutory services then delivered through government offices would eventually become the responsibility of the CRBs. In Vancouver, however, statutory and non-statutory services were already integrated under the VRB. It was anticipated that this experiment in Vancouver would eventually allow other CRBs to control statutory services throughout the province.

During the NDP tenure from 1972 to 1974, grants to community-based organizations increased from $242,678 in 1971-2 to $9.3 million in 1974-5 (BC Ministry of Human Resources 1975). The Ministry of Human Resources budget increased from $148.5 million in 1971-2 to $367.4 million in 1974-5. This era introduced a new phase of government involvement in personal social services. Not only did government become a major funding source for social services, but it also created a large number of jobs (Macdonald 1984). The infusion of funds through the Community Grants Program allowed important social service program developments during the period. Current services and programs that can trace their origins to the early 1970s include youth services, homemaking services, crisis centres, counselling, family services, community information, multi-service centres, and services for groups with special needs.

Macdonald (1984) notes that the NDP government also expanded government-delivered services. In the field of child welfare, social work teams in Vancouver included child care workers and community development workers. In the non-metropolitan areas, district supervisors were authorized to contract with non-profit agencies for these types of workers to provide special services to children: specialized child care services for children living at home and at risk. Services to children in care were also expanded. The government operated group homes for children in care in Vancouver but they were contracted out to non-profit and private groups in the non-metropolitan areas.

Contracting arrangements for the delivery of statutory services in the early 1970s represent the genesis of today's contracting arrangements between government and the voluntary sector. The contracting mode of service delivery caused hardly a ripple at the time, however, because NDP government ideology supported the idea of fostering new service initiatives in the community. In addition, voluntary agencies welcomed these additional resources. It is important to point out that the NDP strategy of routing service delivery through community-based structures contradicted ideologies on the left that favour government delivery. It did appeal, however, to those who saw the monopoly by government and the established agencies as bureaucratic and unresponsive to local needs. Government therefore provided funding to voluntary agencies to develop services and extend them to 'finer shades.' At the same time, it encouraged the development of the public agent role through the contracting process.

The NDP chose to route delivery of these social services through existing and newly emerging community-based organizations instead of a decentralized government structure. The Community Grants Program became the primary mechanism for fostering social services at the local level. Voluntary agencies were encouraged to develop and deliver non-statutory preventive and remedial services, which would eventually become integrated with the statutory services under the CRBs. They were also accountable to the CRBs for the receipt and expenditure of grants. The long-term prospects of the voluntary agencies was less clear: whether funding would be sustained and whether services would remain in the voluntary sector or be absorbed by government, particularly where these services gained province-wide applicability.

In 1975, the Social Credit party was returned to power. It dismantled the Community Resources Boards. Their function of allocating funds from the Community Grants Program was incorporated into the regional offices of the Ministry of Social Services (MSS). Eligibility for Community Grants funding was tightened: funded services had to be eligible as well for cost-shared federal funding and staffed by volunteers. Information centres, transition houses, and community development projects were no longer eligible for such funding. In 1976, a new Family and Child Services Act was passed. It narrowed the government mandate to protection of children, and the act authorized social services to families and children only when children were at risk of being apprehended because of 'exceptional physical, social or behaviourial needs.'

Despite a much more conservative attitude toward welfare on the part of the Social Credit government, researchers note that MSS continued to expand during the late 1970s and early 1980s (Macdonald 1984; Callahan and McNiven 1988). The ministry initially increased its responsibility by assuming the delivery of those services that had come under the dismantled CRBs, for example, especially in the Vancouver area, where the CAS and CCAS had a long history in developing child welfare services. Consequently, Vancouver had a better and more developed range of human care services than the non-metropolitan communities. In the late 1970s, the government added to the range of services by introducing family support workers, child abuse teams, community-based preventive services for juvenile offenders, and special services to handicapped children to facilitate community living. Major service programs that had been initiated by the NDP government continued to be maintained. Contracted services, which had been introduced by the NDP, continued to be an integral part of service delivery. Generally speaking,

> the period from August 1972 to July 1983 was characterized by the expansion and consolidation of social services in British Columbia, delivered both at the public and private levels. While the Social Credit government jettisoned the community resources board experiment which had stimulated expansion of government community grants, the more centralized and bureaucratized system which followed continued government funding for community grants, albeit at more modest and selective levels (Macdonald 1984:9).

In 1983, however, the conservative outlook of the government became manifest when the province was faced with a major reduction in its revenues. The need for budget cutbacks provided an opportunity to put conservative ideas into practice. Less government and lower expenditures were to become familiar refrains in annual budget speeches (BC Ministry of Finance 1983a, 1984a, 1985a; BC Ministry of Finance and Corporate Relations 1986a). Lower expenditures were to be achieved through privatization.

The privatization strategies of the Social Credit government have prompted a resurgence of interest in the potential of the voluntary sector. While the Social Credit government's measures may seem similar to those of the NDP, there are important differences. The NDP government attempted to integrate statutory and non-statutory services through the CRBs. It used the grants mechanism to foster the development of non-statutory services, and delivery of these services was routed though voluntary agencies accountable to the elected CRBs. The boards set priorities and allocated community grants for such services. In contrast, the Social Credit administration curtailed funding for nonstatutory and preventative services. It limited its own direct service role to child protection, adoption, and income assistance, and increasingly contracted with community-based agencies to provide statutory and related services. As mentioned above, revisions to the ministry's mandate depend on the extent to which new legislation enshrines the recommendations from the Community Panel reports.

The 1980s heralded a new era of voluntary sector-government collaboration. As mentioned above, contracting out is not a new phenomenon in British Columbia. The two children's aid societies clearly had an agent relationship with government going back to the 1920s. Contracting out was an integral part of service delivery during the NDP administration in the early 1970s when non-profit societies, under contract with government, hired child care workers to provide special services to children. The expansion of group homes for children coming into care was also contracted out in regions outside the Lower Mainland. Since 1983, however, contracting out has become the modus operandi of government. Voluntary agencies no longer operate according to either the parallel bars or extension ladder models, in which their role is considered marginal to the public sector. They have now assumed an important and an integral role in service delivery. The next chapters examine some of the implications of this for the voluntary sector.

Summary

This brief overview shows that the roots of government-voluntary sector collaboration, currently referred to as a 'partnership' can be traced to the beginnings of the social welfare system in British Columbia. The role of charities and private societies at the turn of the century could be said to fit the parallel bars model of social welfare, in which voluntary organizations provide services parallel to those of government but for a different clientele.

With the expansion of federal and provincial government responsibility for social welfare in the 1950s and 1960s, the foundations of an enforced minimum standard of life were established, and the role of voluntary agencies evolved to fit the extension ladder model. Throughout the period a public agent relationship was forged between the provincial government and the children's aid societies in Vancouver and Victoria, which received almost all their funding from government and provided services to children under statutory authority.

In the 1960s and 1970s, voluntary organizations grew rapidly in direct response to available government funding. Funding came first from federally sponsored job creation projects, and then from the provincial government as it tried to integrate government-provided statutory services with non-statutory services provided by the voluntary sector.

The partnership forged between the two sectors was redefined in the 1980s, when use of purchase-of-service contracts accelerated rapidly. Through such contracts third parties, including voluntary agencies, deliver services on behalf of government and play an integral part in service provision.

3
The Changing Relationship between Government and the Voluntary Sector

Even though our historical overview suggests that government-voluntary sector collaboration in the social services can be traced back to the nineteenth century, the collaboration is difficult to quantify. Particularly difficult to establish is the history of public funding for the voluntary sector. No data are available on how private and non-profit agencies have been linked to the public or government sector, either in the flow of funds or in the allocation of responsibilities between these sectors. Even those who work in the social services system do not always have a clear picture of how the system is financed. Yet it is clear that the more governments use these agencies, both as instruments of social policy and to deliver services on their behalf, the more crucial it is to monitor the funding that links the various sectors.

This chapter addresses three components of the relationship between government and non-profit agencies: (1) the public sector's role in funding and delivering social services; (2) the share of public funds going to private non-profit agencies to enlist them in the delivery of social services; and (3) the ability of the private non-profit sector to respond to increasing social service needs. Since the aim of the Social Credit government was to roll back the public sector to make way for the private sector, it is important to establish whether the non-profit sector can fill in the gaps that may arise from decreased government funding. The amount and type of private and charitable funds received by these agencies can have important implications for the growth and development of the sector. These issues form the basis of the chapter.

Two sources of privatization data are analyzed in the text. Government expenditure trends are based on published sources, while voluntary sector data are based on a province-wide survey of 133 non-profit agencies, lasting from fiscal year 1982-3 to fiscal year 1988-9. Tracking provincial government expenditure on contracts for all ministries over this period proved to be an impossible task. Unlike data available from the Ministry of Social Services (MSS),[1] expenditure on contracted-out services in the other ministries was classified and embedded within direct service programs, making the information impossible to extract. Thus, the analysis of government expenditure trends is limited to published data available for MSS.

It should be noted that even within MSS, funding is difficult to unravel. The components of major program areas are not always consistently classified. Expenditures on Opportunities to Independence (a sub-program within Rehabilitation and Support Services), for example, were classified under Guaranteed Annual Income for Need (GAIN) from 1986-7 on. Similarly, Pharmacare expenditures were included under the MSS budget until 1986-7, when they were transferred to the Ministry of Health. To the extent possible, the following discussion of MSS expenditure trends is based on consistent classification of the estimates available in *Public Accounts of British Columbia* (BC Ministry of Finance 1982-5, BC Ministry of Finance and Corporate Relations 1986-9).

The 133 surveyed non-profit agencies provided information on funding received from all levels of government, as well as philanthropic and charitable giving. The list from which they were chosen was provided by MSS,[2] meaning that all the agencies sampled had received funding from the ministry. MSS is also the government ministry most extensively involved in contracting out.[3] The Ministry of Health and the Ministry of the Attorney General[4] also provide funding for services to families and children and are therefore of interest in this discussion.

MSS limits direct provision to the mandatory responsibilities of income maintenance and child protection. All other services within MSS programs are contracted out. The ministry mandate is to provide the most vulnerable or disadvantaged people in the province with the tools to participate in community life. Those receiving assistance include the long-term and temporarily unemployed, low income earners, families who are experiencing difficulties, children and adults with mental handicaps, senior citizens, and children in need of suitable guardians. The programs can be divided into several types: income assistance, services to help individuals find or retain employment, services to support families to ensure the well-being of children, rehabilitation programs for persons with mental handicaps, and services for seniors.

The mandate of the Ministry of Health is to provide the residents of British Columbia with an efficient, effective, and affordable health care system that promotes an optimum state of health and provides access to an appropriate range of health services. This ministry is organized into several divisions, such as Community and Family Health, Institutional Services, and the Medical Services Commission, among others. Under each division are different branches. Thus, Community and Family Health has the Mental Health Services Branch, Family Health Branch, and so on. Each branch represents a specialized service and has a separate mission statement. The extent of contracting out varies, and expenditures for it are blended with those for direct services.

The Ministry of the Attorney General is organized into nine major branches: Criminal Justice, Court Services, Motor Vehicle, Corrections, Legal Services, Management Services, Police Services, Liquor Distribution, and the Community Justice Branch. The Community Justice Branch was created in 1993 and consolidates all services that are delivered by private individuals and organizations as well as non-profit societies under purchase-of-service contract agreements or grant funding. These services include: Family Maintenance, Wife Assault, Victim Assault, Police Victim Assault, Legal Aid, Alternate Dispute Resolution/Maintenance, Native Courtwork and Counselling, Crime Prevention and Criminal Gangs, and other services that receive core funding. Prior to the establishment of the Community Justice Branch, these services were located under the different branches, and expenditures were also embedded within direct service programs making them difficult to extract.[5]

MSS Expenditure Trends
As has been seen, the role of the organized voluntary sector in social service delivery has increased and the government's role has diminished. Both welfare pluralists and the New Right support this trend, but there are crucial differences between them on the issues of public finance and reliance on informal care. MSS expenditures can be analyzed with their two points of view in mind. Welfare pluralists wish to see the shift in responsibility to the voluntary sector accompanied by a transfer of resources equivalent to what would be spent in direct government provision, to meet 'at least the standards of coverage, responsibility, distribution, quality and access met by them' (Brenton 1985:4). The New Right believes that delegation of social services to the voluntary sector should diminish the state role in both delivery and financing. The New Right's call for a minimal state and a return of

responsibility to individuals and families implies a greater reliance on unpaid informal care. Thus the following data must be assessed to answer the question of whether government spending for contracted-out services has in fact decreased, given that expenditure reduction was one of the declared objectives of Social Credit privatization strategies at the beginning of the 1980s. Under the circumstances defined by the New Right, delegation of responsibility to the voluntary sector would in effect constitute a dismantling of the social services.

Figure 3.1 shows trend lines[6] summarizing actual expenditures (adjusted for inflation) by the three major service program areas in MSS: Rehabilitation and Support Services, Direct Community Services and Administration and Support, and Family and Children's Services.[7] A fourth trend line is included in order to show spending on Rehabilitation and Support Services both including and excluding government expenditures on government-staffed institutions such as Tranquille, Woodlands, and Glendale Lodge, which provide services to mentally handicapped people.[8] The trend lines are based on Table 3.1.

In Figure 3.1, expenditures on Direct Community Services and Administration and Support have been combined. This trend line represents ministry expenditures on its operations and staff in Victoria and in regional and district offices. Spending shows an upward trend with the exception of 1983-4, when government provision of family support workers and the child abuse teams was eliminated and its twenty-two children-in-care resources in Vancouver were contracted out under the new restraint program.

Family and Children's Services include family support services, child care services, and residential services for children in care. The services in this program area have always been contracted out. Funding was reduced to $80.2 million in 1983-4 from $83.9 million in 1982-3, again showing the impact of restraint. Since 1983-4, spending in this program area has shown a general upward trend, with a greater infusion of money in 1987-8. The infusion of money in 1984-5 can be attributed to the contracting out of twenty-two ministry-operated group homes in Vancouver, which shifted the expenditure from Direct Community Services to Family and Children's Services. This decrease in one area and increase in the other is reflected in the same year if expenditure on Family and Children's Services is compared to that of Direct Community Services. This reflection is not shown in Figure 3.1 because the expenditure on Direct Community Services is combined with expenditure on Administration and Support.

Table 3.1

Summary of annual expenditures by major program classification, MSS, 1982-3 to 1988-9 (millions of dollars, inflation adjusted, 1982 = 100)

Fiscal year	GAIN	Rehabilitation and Support[2,3]	Family and Children's Services[1]	Services to Seniors	Direct Community Services	Administration and Support	Housing	Pharmacare	Total
1982-3	640.3	121.3 (63.1)	83.9	33.8	77.8	44.4	–	90.8	1,092.3
1983-4	768.9	134.3 (77.4)	80.2	30.7	89.7	22.0	–	100.6	1,226.4
1984-5	810.9	139.3 (87.0)	87.3	27.1	87.9	31.8	–	108.4	1,292.7
1985-6	812.9	132.8 (91.0)	89.2	25.9	88.0	28.3	–	120.7	1,297.8
1986-7	762.2	130.8 (86.0)	88.2	25.0	90.8	31.8	–	140.4	1,269.2
1987-8	746.1	134.3 (83.5)	96.7	27.5	92.3	34.6	13.6	–	1,145.1
1988-9	723.1	147.9 (97.2)[4]	93.2	27.2	98.5	39.0	15.6	–	1,444.5

Source: BC Ministry of Finance, *Public Accounts of British Columbia* (Victoria: Ministry of Finance 1982-5); BC Ministry of Finance and Corporate Relations, *Accounts of British Columbia* (Victoria: Ministry of Finance and Corporate Relations 1986-9)

Note: The same categories of data, when taken from the MSS *Annual Reports*, show slight discrepancies in the numbers. See Table A.3.

[1] Net of recoveries received from the federal government in the form of Family Allowance payments for children-in-care.

[2] Net of recoveries received from the Medical Services Plan for salaries and sessional medical services.

[3] Beginning in 1986-7 funding for Opportunities to Independence was transferred from Rehabilitation and Support Services to GAIN. For consistency this funding has been added to Rehabilitation and Support Services in this table.

[4] Figures in brackets represent Rehabilitation and Support minus spending on institutional care, i.e., expenditure on Woodlands, Tranquille, Glendale Lodge and Alder Lodge.

Figure 3.1

Expenditure trends by major program classification, MSS, 1982-3 to 1988-9 (millions of dollars, inflation adjusted, 1982=100)

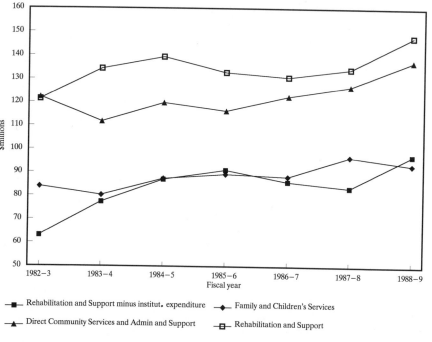

— ■ — Rehabilitation and Support minus institut. expenditure — ◆ — Family and Children's Services

— ▲ — Direct Community Services and Admin and Support — □ — Rehabilitation and Support

MSS spending on Rehabilitation and Support Services[9] is interesting because it shows the effects of both deinstitutionalization and privatization. Tranquille[10] was closed in 1984, and the expenditure trend line shows that there was a substantial decline in aggregate government spending in 1985-6 and 1986-7, followed by an upward trend signifying growth in expenditure. A trend line that excludes all expenditures on government-operated institutions is included to show whether transfers equivalent to what was spent when these resources were operated by the ministry were made to alternative and community-based programs. Excluding expenditures on Tranquille, Woodlands,[11] and Glendale Lodge,[12] this trend line shows an initial spurt in spending in 1985-6, followed by a decline until 1987-8. It was only in 1988-9 that government expenditure levels became higher than they were in 1984-5.

The results for Rehabilitation and Support Services raise several questions. The two trend lines show that aggregate expenditure declined with the closure of Tranquille. Although there was some increase in funding to alternative and community-based programs following this closure, the results show that this transfer was obviously not equivalent to what was spent before Tranquille was closed. The initial decline of MSS expenditures (which remained below the 1984-5 level until 1988-9) raises questions about the adequacy of services in terms of number and types of services, as well as the quality and standard of services for those who were deinstitutionalized from large government-run resources. The central question is whether community-based alternatives can provide services of the same quality and acceptability as government-run services, at a lower cost. Can they do so given their level of funding? Without adequate and appropriate services, deinstitutionalization may well result in clients exchanging one form of incarceration for another.

In 1988-9, four years after the closure of Tranquille, MSS expenditure on Rehabilitation and Support Services was slightly higher than the 1984-5 level. It is possible that there was a four-year lag while community-based programs were established. The data prompt us to ask what happened to newly diagnosed clients and clients who had never been institutionalized in terms of the calibre and extent of service provided in the four-year interim. Given that a larger number of clients in 1988-9 (deinstitutionalized clients, as well as new clients who were never institutionalized) received services funded at slightly more than the 1984-5 level, it is important to discover whether the contracted-out community-based programs have replaced like with like in their substitution for government services. The alternative is that without an adequate transfer of resources, these community-based alternatives offer services of a reduced quality. Shragge (1990) argues that community-based alternatives often cost less than the public sector because of low wages and an absence of management structures. Implicit political belief in the cost-effectiveness of the voluntary sector allows the government to gradually reduce its expenditures while sustaining the illusion that the issue of standards has been addressed.

Each of the three program areas demonstrates an increase in funding in the seven-year period considered.[13] Spending on Direct Community Services and Administration and Support shows a gradual increase even though we know that during this period MSS moved to limit its activities to the purely statutory responsibilities of child protection and income maintenance. This contradicts claims that restraint and privatization would lead to less government. Expenditure on Family and Children's Services increased by $10 million in the seven-year period under study. It is difficult, however, to assess whether this expenditure is equivalent to what would have been spent if government were to provide these services directly. Since the services have always been contracted out, it is not possible to compare expenditure on them to the expense of a system in which they are delivered through a decentralized government structure. For Rehabilitation and Support Services, the data showed that the closure of government-staffed institutions was not initially accompanied by expenditures equivalent to what was spent before resources were closed. There was an upward trend in spending in 1988-9, when expenditures slightly exceeded the 1984-5 levels.

While government appears to have maintained an upward spending pattern, a more detailed analysis of expenditure patterns against contextual data is required. The issues of adequacy and standards also need to be addressed. It is therefore necessary to gather data on the number of children coming into care, the number who would be in care but are given different services because of changing philosophies, the increase in child neglect and abuse, the number of families unemployed, and so on. The annual reports published by MSS, for example, show that the number of children coming into care is declining. While this finding points to real increases in the government expenditure shown above, it raises other questions. Is the decline related to a changed idea of when children should come into care? Do the children currently in care need more intensive and therefore more expensive services? What has happened to clients who might formerly have come into care? Similarly, to make sense of spending in Rehabilitation and Support Services, more data are required on the number of clients from Tranquille and Woodlands who were placed in the community, the number of clients who have never been in institutions, the kinds of services required by these clients, and so on.

The contextual data required for such an analysis are not easily accessible,[14] and a much more simplified analysis of per capita expenditures[15] is therefore presented in Table 3.2. The table shows that per capita expenditures have either been maintained or increased for Rehabilitation and Support Services, Family and Children's Services, and Direct Community Services. Spending on Administration and Support declined from $15.9 per capita in 1982-3 to $13.1 in 1988-9, but it is not clear whether the decrease can be attributed to reclassification of some expenditures from this category to Direct Community Services. Per capita expenditures (based on both the total of all categories and the total excluding expenditures on Housing and Pharmacare) increased until 1984-5 but have been decreasing since then, although the 1988-9 level is above that of 1982-3. GAIN payments, which vary according to upswings and downswings in the economy, make up a substantial component of these expenditures.

The rationale for privatization in British Columbia was both fiscal and political. From the government's point of view, restraint was necessary because of declining revenues. Less government and lower expenditures were to be achieved by allowing the private sector to take over functions and activities not appropriate to government. The above results indicate that government spending has continued to increase, although it could be argued that the pace of increase has been much slower since 1985-6 compared to the period before. It is possible that the rhetoric of restraint and privatization enabled government to adopt a service delivery strategy that slowed down the pace of increase of government spending. Downswings in the economy, accompanied by demands on services, may make it more difficult to implement stringent cost-saving strategies. Government may also have little choice if it is mandated to provide these services.

The Finances of the Voluntary Sector
Writings on the voluntary sector generally assume a popular understanding of the term and use it to refer to all extragovernmental activity. This is not a very useful reference point as it covers numerous associations that vary in type, activity, history, size, and level of organization. Hatch (1980) argues that the great diversity of voluntary organizations makes it difficult to ask meaningful questions about them as a group. Formulating a typology to facilitate research in this area is therefore hampered by the difficulty of clearly defining voluntary organizations.

Attempts to formulate a definition generally begin by examining the boundaries between different types of organizations. A distinction is usually made between the informal, the voluntary, the statutory or governmental, and the for-profit sectors for meeting social needs (Wolfenden Committee 1978). Hatch defines voluntary organizations as '(i) being organizations, not informal groups; (ii) not established by statute or under statutory authority and not controlled by statutory authority; and (iii) not commercial in the sense of being profit making or, like much of the private sector in health and education, being mainly dependent for their resources on fees and charges paid by private individuals' (Hatch 1980:15). For the purposes of this inquiry, the term voluntary organization refers to organized forms of social endeavour

Table 3.2

Per capita expenditures[1] by major program classification, MSS, 1982-3 to 1988-9 (inflation adjusted, 1982=100)

Fiscal year	GAIN	Rehabilitation and Support	Family and Children's Services	Services to Seniors	Direct Community Services	Administration and Support	Total[2]
1982-3	229.7	43.5 (22.6)	30.1	12.1	27.9	15.9	391.0 (359.2)
1983-4	273.3	47.8 (27.5)	28.5	10.9	31.9	7.82	435.8 (400.1)
1984-5	284.9	48.9 (30.6)	30.7	9.5	30.9	11.2	454.1 (415.9)
1985-6	283.2	46.3 (31.7)	31.1	9.0	30.7	9.9	452.0 (410.4)
1986-7	263.8	45.3 (29.8)	30.5	8.7	31.4	11.0	439.3 (390.3)
1987-8	255.1	45.9 (28.5)	33.0	9.4	31.5	11.8	391.3 (386.7)
1988-9	$242.3	$49.6 (32.6)[3]	$31.2	$9.1	$33.0	$13.1	$383.5 (378.3)[4]

[1] Provincial population 1982 to 1988 obtained from Research Office, MSS.
[2] Totals include expenditure on housing and Pharmacare, for which per capita expenditures are not shown.
[3] Dollar figures in brackets represent Rehabilitation and Support minus spending on institutional care, i.e., expenditure on Woodlands, Tranquille, Glendale Lodge, and Alder Lodge.
[4] Dollar figures in brackets represent per capita expenditures based on total expenditure minus that spent on housing and Pharmacare.

carried out by non-profit societies which may or may not be registered charities. They have a shape and form and a division of labour. This latter characteristic distinguishes voluntary organizations from the informal system of exchange between relatives, friends and neighbours, and self-help groups that makes up the bulk of caring in our society.

Johnson (1981:20) reviews a number of attempts to classify voluntary social agencies and concludes that 'no single typology is likely to be appropriate for all purposes, and the one selected in particular instances will depend on the questions asked.' Brenton (1985) argues that in examining the role of the voluntary sector in providing welfare services, it is important to understand what these organizations do. Categorization by function does not eliminate the difficulty of classifying multi-form and multi-purpose organizations into mutually exclusive groups, but it is usually possible to distinguish between organizations by some major defining function. Brenton extends the classifications by function offered by Johnson (1981) and Murray (1969), and suggests the following typology:

– the service providing function
– the mutual aid function
– the pressure group function
– the resource function
– the coordinating function (Brenton 1985:11)

This text concentrates on voluntary agencies that can be classified under the service-providing function – provision of a direct service to the public – such as information, advice, support, or counselling. These services may be delivered by paid employees, who may or may not be professionals, or volunteers. This category of agencies is most likely to have equivalents in the public sector and to work in concert with them. The function of voluntary agencies at the local level may differ from that of their parent organization. At the latter level voluntary organizations appear to be most structured and formal, and may act as a liaison or coordinating agent between small local bodies engaged in a variety of functions.

It is important to be aware of the sources of funding and different proportions of funds from respective sources in order to understand the evolution and present state of the relationship between the voluntary sector and the government. Funding patterns explain the extent to which voluntary organizations are independent of government funding, which also has important implications for their ability to fill in service gaps in the face of government cutbacks. The following sections review the revenue sources of the 133 voluntary agencies surveyed. The period covered extends from the 1982-3 fiscal year to 1988-9 inclusive.

Table 3.3 shows the sources of funding for the 133 agencies. Funding from all federal, provincial, and municipal government sources represented approximately 80 per cent of the total agency budgets in the fiscal years 1982-3 and 1988-9. Nongovernment sources of funding represented about 20 per cent of total funding in both years. The importance of provincial government support to these agencies should be noted. Particularly important is the change in provincial government grant and contract funding. The proportion of provincial contract funding, for example, rose from 39.4 per cent to 52.2 per cent, and the amount rose by 137.7 per cent; whereas the proportion of provincial grant funding dropped from 34.8 per cent to 21.4 per cent, but its amount rose by 10.4 per cent.

Table 3.3

Percentage distribution and percentage change in different sources of funding for 133 non-profit agencies (in thousands of dollars, inflation adjusted, 1982=100)

	Fiscal year 1982-3	% of total	Fiscal year 1988-9	% of total	% change 1982-3 to 1988-9
All govt. sources	50,714	79.0	91,362	79.3	+80.2
Prov. govt. grants	22,375	34.8	24,702	21.4	+10.4
Prov. govt. contracts	25,330	39.4	60,209	52.2	+137.7
Federal govt. funding	2,381	3.7	5,517	4.8	+131.7
Municipal govt. funding	626	1.0	933	0.8	+49.0
Nongovt. sources	13,506	21.0	23,920	20.7	+77.1
United Way	1,422	2.2	1,933	1.7	+35.9
Own fundraising*	3,362	5.2	7,179	6.2	+113.5
Fee-for-service and other charges	8,720	13.7	14,806	12.8	+69.8
Total	64,220	100.0	115,282	100.0	+79.5

* Includes donations, membership fees, and fundraising activities such as casinos, bingos, and special event fundraising.

These findings demonstrate that overall funding from government to voluntary organizations increased significantly over the period. As MSS moved out of direct service provision in 1983 and contracted out its staffed resources, funding was reclassified under contracted-out dollars. Some of the services directly provided by government that had been abolished in the restraint program reappeared as contracted-out dollars and funding was reallocated. There was also some program development in 1988, when $20 million was made available under Initiatives for the Family, and services were contracted out under purchase-of-service contract agreements. Other ministries, such as Attorney General, Health, and Advanced Education also became more involved in purchase-of-service contracting after 1983 (see Table 3.6). These changes are reflected in the trend in funding increases shown in Table 3.3.

Table 3.3 also shows that government and nongovernment sources of funding over the period grew at approximately the same rate (approximately 80 per cent). Within government sources, however, provincial government contracts showed the largest increase (137.7 per cent), followed by federal government funding (131.7 per cent). Within nongovernment sources, funds from agencies' own fundraising and fee-for-service and other charges show the largest increases (113.5 and 69.8 per cent, respectively). The increase in absolute funding from different sources from 1982-3 to 1988-9 is shown in Figure 3.2. The proportions of provincial government funding remained the same in 1982-3 and 1988-9. When provincial government funding is disaggregated into grants and contracts, however, Table 3.3 shows that in 1982-3, grants made up 35 per cent of total funding and contracts made up 39 per cent, whereas by 1988-9, grant funding had declined to 21 per cent, while contract funding had increased to 52 per cent of total funding. Contrary to popular belief, contract funding was larger than grant funding in 1982-3, which shows that contracting was an integral part of service delivery even in the pre-privatization period.

Table 3.4 examines the percentage distribution and percentage change in different sources of income for 97 of the 133 agencies surveyed. The agencies received provincial government funding consistently over the seven-year period under study. Agencies that did not provide consistent data, or that were founded later in the 1980s in response to available government funding, were excluded because they were likely to have contributed to the increase in government funding. The 97 agencies demonstrate that the proportion of government (all three levels) and nongovernment funding was the same in 1982-3 and 1988-9.

Figure 3.2

Trends in government and nongovernment sources of funding for 133 non-profit agencies, 1982-3 to 1988-9 (millions of dollars, inflation adjusted, 1982=100)

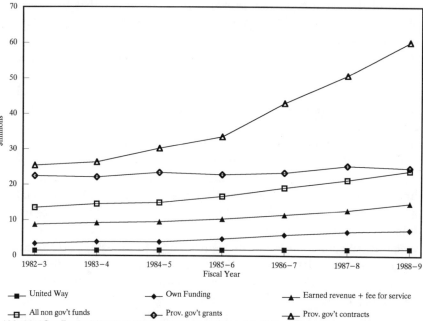

* Municipal Govt Funding is less than a million and hence has not been included in the graph

The proportion of provincial grant funding, however, is much lower than that shown in Table 3.3 in both years, and the proportion of provincial contract funding does not show as marked an increase for 1988-9 as in Table 3.3. The large shift toward contract funding shown in Table 3.3 is possibly explained by the inclusion of newer agencies. When they are removed from Table 3.4, the shift is not nearly so dramatic. As for nongovernment sources of funding in Table 3.4, funds from agencies' own fundraising show the largest change (+140.9 per cent), but fee-for-service and other charges make up the largest share of nongovernmental funding.

Table 3.5 shows variations in sources of non-profit support by size of community.[16] Small communities were more dependent on government sources of funding in the pre-privatization period. In 1988-9, funding from all three levels of government seems to have equalized for different-sized communities. In all regions, provincial government funding was the most important source of funding.

Interestingly, the shift toward contract funding is demonstrated only in the large metropolitan communities. In medium-sized communities the proportion of contract funding rose less steeply over the period, and in small communities it dropped. The extent of contracting out between government and non-profit agencies was much greater in the small and medium-sized communities, however, even in the pre-privatization period. It appears that downsizing and privatization introduced in the early 1980s also brought services in the large metropolitan communities in line with the rest of the province.

Table 3.4

Percentage distribution and percentage change in different sources of funding for 97 non-profit agencies consistently receiving provincial government funding (in thousands of dollars, inflation adjusted, 1982 = 100) from 1982-3 to 1988-9

	Fiscal year 1982-3	% of total	Fiscal year 1988-9	% of total	% change 1982-3 to 1988-9
All govt. sources	32,161	78.5	49,812	77.7	+54.9
Prov. govt. grants	3,989	9.7	4,364	6.8	+9.4
Prov. govt. contracts	25,330	61.8	40,857	63.7	+61.3
Federal govt. funding	2,215	5.4	3,716	5.8	+67.7
Municipal govt. funding	626	1.5	875	1.4	+39.8
Nongovt. sources	8,806	21.5	14,322	22.3	+62.6
United Way	1,183	2.9	1,444	2.3	+22.1
Own fundraising*	1,943	4.7	4,680	7.3	+140.9
Fee-for-service and other charges	5,680	13.9	8,197	12.7	44.3
Total	40,968	100.0	64,136	100.0	+56.6%

* Includes donations, membership, and fundraising from casinos, bingos, and special event fundraising.

As shown in Table 3.5, the proportion of provincial government grant funding is much lower in small and medium-sized communities than in large metropolitan communities in both 1982-3 and 1988-9, and does not change significantly over the period. The larger proportion of grant funding shown for large metropolitan communities may be explained by the fact that most headquarter organizations (such as the Red Cross) are located in Vancouver. They receive funding – categorized by locality – to provide services across the province.

Table 3.5

Percentage distribution of different sources of funding for 133 non-profit agencies, by community size (inflation adjusted, 1982=100)

	Large metropolitan communities[1]		Medium-sized communities[2]		Small-sized communities[3]	
	1982-3	1988-9	1982-3	1988-9	1982-3	1988-9
All govt. sources	78.6	79.5	77.2	78.1	85.8	78.8
Prov. govt. grants	41.2	25.8	4.4	2.9	3.3	2.3
Prov. govt. contracts	33.4	48.0	62.8	69.9	78.7	71.8
Federal govt. funding	3.2	5.0	7.3	3.5	3.8	4.7
Municipal govt. funding	0.8	0.7	2.7	1.8	–	0.1
Nongovt. sources	21.3	20.5	22.8	21.9	14.2	21.1
United Way	2.4	1.9	1.8	1.3	0.1	0.3
Earned revenue	4.9	3.5	2.4	2.6	5.0	5.4
Fee-for-service	7.6	8.2	14.1	7.2	6.3	7.6
Own fundraising	5.7	5.8	4.3	9.8	0.9	4.8
Other	0.7	1.1	0.3	0.9	1.8	3.0
Total	100.0	100.0	100.0	100.0	100.0	100.0

[1] The large metropolitan communities are represented by the Victoria Capital Regional District (CRD) and the Greater Vancouver Regional District (GVRD) as well as Matsqui, Sumas, and Abbotsford, suburban communities that abut the GVRD.
[2] The medium-sized communities are represented by Prince George, Kelowna, Kamloops, and Nanaimo.
[3] Cranbrook, Nelson, Dawson Creek, Quesnel, and Terrace represent the small-sized communities.

Nongovernment sources of funding increased from 14.2 per cent in 1982-3 to 21.1 per cent in 1988-9 in small communities, and made up approximately 20 per cent of total funding in both large and medium-sized communities in both fiscal years. Funds from agencies' own fundraising (usually from gaming and casinos) showed a dramatic increase in small and medium-sized communities, but remained the same in the large metropolitan communities. The proportion of United Way funding declined, remaining a small proportion of total budgets in all communities.

These data demonstrate that the provincial government is the most important source of funding for non-profit agencies. The non-profit sector's role in delivering non-statutory preventative social services has been declining since 1975, when the Social Credit party was returned to power. Agencies were given a new lease on life, however, with the expansion of contract funding during the period under study. During the 1980s, they increasingly delivered statutory and statutory-related services on behalf of government, and provincial government funding was the fastest-growing source of funding available to them. The NDP government has continued with the purchase-of-service contracting model. However, it has also made global funding available to advocacy and women's groups. The extent to which it will move to fund the more preventative services will depend on whether the Panel Report recommendations are enshrined in new legislation. Although it tends to be believed that non-profit organizations have traditionally relied on donations as their primary source of revenue, the findings of this study suggest otherwise.

Without this scale of government support, it is questionable whether voluntary agencies could continue with many of the essential services they currently provide. Admittedly, revenues from their own fundraising efforts have increased dramatically, but these cannot be expected to reach the level of government funding. Private sources of income cannot replace government support of the non-profit sector, and it is unrealistic to expect that the private sector will fill in the gaps should government reduce its funding. The perception that the accomplishments and success of the voluntary sector are based on private effort may create a climate in which it is politically easy for governments to reduce their support of programs administered and delivered by this sector.

These findings raise important questions about the respective social roles of government and non-profit agencies. Agency dependence on government funding underlies an ongoing debate about the autonomy of the sector. As non-profit agencies increasingly rely on and compete for government funding, there is concern that they become more and more responsive to the goals and requirements of the government departments with which they have contracts. The range of potential responses to any given social problem is now more limited given that these organizations traditionally served as alternatives to government provision. When an agency is totally dependent on funds through contracting, it is questionable whether it can still be called voluntary or is, more accurately, quasi-governmental.

The Relationship between Government and Nongovernment Sources of Funding
An examination of data clearly reveals the trend toward contracting out of social services. Table 3.6 shows the average number of contracts per voluntary agency by the listed ministries for each of four periods from the 1960s onward, and also the overall average for each ministry. Executive directors of the 133 agencies were asked to verify the start dates of their current contracts. The table shows that the average number of contracts given out by every ministry increased markedly in the post-privatization period.

Table 3.6

Mean number of ministry contracts started in the different decades by non-profit agencies

Ministry awarding contract	1960s	1970s	1980-3	1984-9	Overall
MSS (96 agencies)	.30	.81	.59	2.2	3.9
Health (55 agencies)	.21	.90	.12	1.3	2.6
Attorney general (30 agencies)	.00	.47	.23	1.4	2.1
Other prov. ministries (24 agencies)	.16	.33	.17	.72	1.3

The seven-year budget data collected from the surveyed agencies were collapsed to compare pre- and post-privatization periods.[17] Although the provincial government officially announced its privatization policy during the 1983-4 fiscal year, examination of its departmental data suggests that the policy was not implemented until

1984-5 and that it was then reflected in the 1985-6 budget of the agencies surveyed (see Figure 3.2). These data trends provided the rationale for defining the pre- and post-privatization periods for the analysis presented here.[18]

All voluntary agencies were expected to receive provincial government grant and contract funding. Table 3.7, however, shows that ten agencies (10.3 per cent) received only grant funding, forty-four (45.4 per cent) received only contract funding, and forty-three (44.3 per cent) received both grant and contract funding.[19] For the ten agencies receiving only grant funding from the provincial government, this source made up 30 and 32 per cent of total funding in the pre- and post-privatization periods, respectively. These were small agencies in that the average provincial government grant received in the pre- and post-privatization periods was approximately $25,500 and $42,200 respectively (an increase of 65 per cent). It is not clear from the data whether these agencies made a deliberate decision not to pursue contracting or whether they were unsuccessful in their quest to do so. Their total funding from nongovernmental sources amounted to 52 per cent in the pre-privatization period and 54 per cent in the post-privatization period.

The forty-four agencies that received only contract funding from the provincial government marginally increased their reliance on such funding in the post-privatization period from 71 to 72 per cent. The average contract dollars received by these agencies increased by 31 per cent, however, from $325,600 per agency in the pre-privatization period to $426,200 per agency in the post-privatization period. Funding from the three levels of government made up approximately 80 per cent of total funding, compared to 20 per cent from nongovernment sources, for both the pre- and post-privatization periods.

For the forty-three agencies receiving both grant and contract funding from the provincial government, the proportion of contract funding increased marginally in the post-privatization period from 56 to 58 per cent. The average contract funding received by these agencies increased from $284,400 per agency before privatization to $374,200 per agency after privatization, an increase of 31 per cent. The proportion, as well as the average amount, of provincial government grant funding to these agencies decreased in the post-privatization period. Combining grants and contracts, provincial government funding made up approximately 70 per cent of the total funding of these agencies in both the pre- and post-privatization periods. As in the case of agencies

Table 3.7

Proportion of different sources of funding, by type of provincial funding in the pre- and post-privatization periods (in thousands of dollars, inflation adjusted, 1982=100)

	Prov. contract	Prov. grants	Total prov. funding	Total govt. funding*	Nongov't funding
	Total funding	Total funding	Total funding	Total funding	Total funding
Agencies receiving prov. grants (10)					
Pre-privatization	–	30% (x̄=25.5)	30%	48%	52%
Post-privatization	–	32 (x̄=42.2)	32	46	54
Agencies receiving prov. contracts (44)					
Pre-privatization	71% (x̄=325.6)	–	71	79	21
Post-privatization	72 (x̄=426.2)	–	72	78	22
Agencies receiving prov. grants and contracts (43)					
Pre-privatization	56 (x̄=284.4)	16 (x̄=81.8)	72	79	21
Post privatization	58 (x̄=374.2)	12 (x̄=75.1)	70	78	22

Note: x̄=mean or average funding from that source per agency, in $1000s.
* Includes federal, provincial & municipal government funding.

receiving contract funding only, funding from all three levels of government made up approximately 80 per cent of the total funding in both periods, and nongovernment sources of income made up approximately 20 per cent.

The above results reveal that contract funding in the post-privatization period was increasingly important only to those agencies receiving both grants and contracts from the provincial government. Grants declined as a proportion of total funding, as did the average amount of such funding. It should also be noted that the average grant amount received by these agencies is much smaller than the average contract amount. Agencies that received only provincial grant funding tended to be smaller and to rely more heavily on nongovernmental sources of income. The ratio of nongovernment funding for these agencies remained at over 50 per cent in both periods. It follows therefore that the client group served and the services provided by these agencies were more likely different from those served and provided by the other agencies. Agencies that received only contract funding, on the other hand, were similar to agencies that received both grant and contract funding from the provincial government. Provincial government funding made up approximately 70 per cent of the total funding of these agencies, other government sources (municipal and federal) contributed another 10 per cent, and nongovernment sources constituted the remaining 20 per cent.

The results suggest that non-profit agencies that contract with government to provide services tend to be larger than others and are more likely to increase in size. They are less dependent than small agencies on nongovernment sources of income. It is possible that the economies in scale in contracting, or the substantial amount of government funding received by agencies, eases the pressure to raise funds. The greater the number of contracts or projects, the lower the overhead, since the average operating cost declines as agencies undertake many more contracts. Significant savings in operating costs can be attained by increasing the size as well as the number of contracts. The savings can then be used to pay for administration and to provide other services considered important by the agency. This possibility may be one explanation of the finding by researchers such as Kramer (1986) that the agency role does not appear to interfere with autonomy. Another possibility is that these agencies are becoming more like government departments, with a resulting congruence between contracted services and services defined under the mission statement.

Table 3.8 further disaggregates the data in Table 3.7 in order to examine the relationship between provincial government funding and nongovernment sources of funding.[20] Even though disaggregration leads to small numbers in some categories, the table shows that if agencies relied on either grants or contracts and that funding then declined, a marked growth in nongovernment sources of funding ensued. Thus, a decline from 26 to 14 per cent in the proportion of provincial government funding for agencies receiving grants only was accompanied by an increase in nongovernment funding from 58 to 71 per cent in the pre- and post-privatization periods. Similarly, agencies demonstrating a decline in provincial government contract funding showed an increase in the proportion of nongovernment funding.

The relationship between government and nongovernment funding can be one indicator of the extent to which the agency maintains control and flexibility in determining its own range of services and activities. Nongovernment sources of funding allow agencies to carry out mission-related activities that may be at variance with the objectives of the government departments with which they contract. As governments increasingly rely on non-profit agencies to deliver services on its behalf, there is concern that in competing for such funding, voluntary agencies become unduly influenced by the needs and requirements of government departments. Non-profit agencies are not likely to receive government funding to provide services and to serve constituencies that do not fall within departmental mandates. When conditions attached to funding are tightly controlled, activities and organizations that do not match government priorities will not survive unless they can find resources elsewhere. It has been observed that 'where government departments have certain statutory responsibilities which must be met from the total amount of money available to them, only limited funds are left over for help to voluntary organizations which are not simply acting on an agency basis to fulfil statutory duties' (Wolfenden Committee 1978: appendix 4). These opposing views regarding the extent to which doing business with government influences the autonomy of these agencies is further explored in Chapter 5.

As mentioned above, MSS, under the Social Credit government, limited its mandate to its statutory responsibilities of income assistance and child protection. The services that it funded through contracts were also more focused on services where children were either in care, or at risk of coming into care. Even clients who requested services directly or through another agency were screened by social workers to see if they

Table 3.8

Proportion of different sources of funding, by type of provincial funding and by its pre- and post-privatization increase or decrease (in thousands of dollars, inflation adjusted, 1982=100)

	Prov. contracts	Prov. grants	Total prov. funding	Total govt. funding*	Nongov't funding
	Total funding	Total funding	Total funding	Total funding	Total funding
Agencies receiving prov. grants (10)					
Grant funding increase (4)					
Pre-privatization		46% ($\bar{x}$=17.8)	46%	75%	25%
Post-privatization		64 ($\bar{x}$=77.5)	64	75	25
Grant funding decrease (6)					
Pre-privatization		26 ($\bar{x}$=30.7)	26	42	58
Post-privatization		14 ($\bar{x}$=18.5)	14	29	71
Agencies receiving prov. contracts (44)					
Contract funding increase (37)					
Pre-privatization	71% ($\bar{x}$=324.0)	–	71	79	21
Post-privatization	72 ($\bar{x}$=456.5)	–	72	79	21

(continued on next page)

Table 3.8 (continued)

	Prov. contracts	Prov. grants	Total prov. funding	Total govt. funding*	Nongov't funding
	Total funding	Total funding	Total funding	Total funding	Total funding
Contract funding decrease (7)					
Pre-privatization	78 ($\bar{x}=334.1$)	–	78	83	17
Post-privatization	69 ($\bar{x}=266.3$)	–	69	73	27
Agencies receiving prov. grants and contracts (43)					
Contracts>Grants (24)					
Pre-privatization	72 ($\bar{x}=482.7$)	3 ($\bar{x}=22.5$)	75	80	20
Post-privatization	71 ($\bar{x}=622.8$)	3 ($\bar{x}=24.0$)	74	79	21
Grants>Contracts (14)					
Pre-privatization	1 ($\bar{x}=3.4$)	59 ($\bar{x}=151.1$)	60	71	29
Post-privatization	5 ($\bar{x}=17.1$)	45 ($\bar{x}=145.7$)	50	72	28
Grants switched to contracts (5)					
Pre-privatization	29 ($\bar{x}=119.4$)	42 ($\bar{x}=172.2$)	71	84	16
Post-privatization	36 ($\bar{x}=180.8$)	25 ($\bar{x}=122.6$)	61	77	23

Note: $\bar{x}$=mean or average funding from that source per agency, in $1000s.
* Includes federal, provincial, and municipal government funding.

met the criteria of eligibility. Voluntary agencies that delivered services under purchase-of-service agreements provided services that focused on government programs and government referred clients. In 1988 some flexibility was introduced when the Social Credit government injected $20 million into the Family Initiative Program. This funding supported services that were more preventative and supportive of families and did not always require MSS social workers to play a gatekeeping role. It is not yet clear what changes will be introduced and implemented by the NDP. The philosophical shift to a family-centred system, the recommendations of the Korbin Report on sectoral bargaining, and the move to involve communities suggest a delivery model requiring an even closer relationship between government and the non-profit sector.

These developments indicate that there is a blurring of roles and responsibilities between government and the organized voluntary sector. This blurring can, in part, be explained by the similarity of their funding. Research by Hollingsworth and Hollingsworth (1986) illustrates the point. The authors compared public hospitals, private hospitals, and voluntary hospitals in the U.S. on a number of measures for three years: 1935, 1961, and 1979. They found that the three hospital types tended to resemble one another over time, and argue that the convergence results from similarity in funding sources. In the earlier period, public hospitals were primarily funded through local and state taxes, voluntary hospitals through philanthropic and charitable giving, and private hospitals through charges to patients. Both the behaviour of the different types of hospital and the constituencies they served were quite different at that time. Recently, with the emergence of third-party reimbursement paid by insurance companies (which tend to be neutral in their choice of hospitals), the distinction between the three sectors has become blurred.

In British Columbia there are no standard rates when government buys services from non-profit agencies, and so the size and number of contracts an agency receives depends on the 'grantsmanship' of its executive director. It is possible that the executive directors of these larger agencies are concentrating their grantsmanship on securing government rather than nongovernment funding, the availability and growth of which are nowhere near those of government sources. The executive directors of larger agencies tend to be well connected politically and are often hired from within the ranks of the public sector. This tendency to hire management staff from within the public sector became fashionable once it became clear that service contracts were becoming the way of doing business with government. The requirements for preparing proposals and complying with government procedures and regulations led the board of directors of many of these agencies to acknowledge that they needed to hire individuals with the know-how to negotiate with government. The larger societies were more likely to be in a financial position to hire executive directors familiar with the professional and administrative subculture operative in government. Many of these initially large agencies are now even larger with budgets of several million dollars.

Agencies that are successful at garnering contracts tend to have a virtual monopoly on services required by government. They have developed the expertise and other necessary resources on which government depends for service delivery to clients who may have a statutory right to that service. Since reimbursement for services is usually bargained between the government (as buyer) and the non-profit agency (as seller), the monopoly exercised by some agencies allows them to bargain at higher rates compared to smaller agencies.

However, because of the lack of standard rates there can be disagreements between what government is prepared to pay and the agency's estimate of the true cost of providing a service. Agencies may accept what government is prepared to pay because its survival may be threatened. It may also not want the contracts to be awarded to what it perceives as a lesser or competing agency, or the private sector. Agencies that attempt to bargain at rates that reflect the real cost of providing a service face a dilemma in that they may price themselves out of the system. Agencies that attempt to factor their mission-related activities into cost may seem expensive and further encourage government to seek out other service providers. Kramer (1981) has also pointed out that it is only when the voluntary sector begins to charge rates that reflect market costs that this arena becomes attractive to the for-profit sector. He notes that there are obvious cost advantages to government using voluntary agencies to deliver services on its behalf. When there is no cost advantage, government may want to take over and administer programs directly.

Agencies that have not developed the grantsmanship, or are new to service delivery, may negotiate a low rate with government that does not cover the actual cost of service. Such agencies must make up the recurring deficit by seeking additional funding from other sources. Smaller agencies that are struggling to maintain a shoestring operation may have to contend with high staff turnover, recruitment, and other problems that reflect the ever-present threat of loss of funding. Having to rely on other funds to cover government funding shortfalls often leads to claims that the purchase-of-service contracting model enables government to download its responsibilities and that the voluntary sector is subsidizing government services. There does not appear to be any clear government policy articulating whether non-profit agencies are expected to charge less than the expected cost and make up the difference by seeking contributions from private sources. The interviews with the executive directors gave the impression that there was tremendous variation in practice between different ministries and between regional and local offices within ministries.

Older, established voluntary agencies are already focused on ministry programs, are managing many contracts, are successful at grantsmanship from other sources, and are able to negotiate better rates than smaller agencies. Newer and smaller agencies may lack the staff and expertise to deal with complex government systems. They are more likely to experience problems because their future depends on voluntary and charitable giving, which are unpredictable.

Such disparities in the way that different non-profit organizations fare over contract funding can hinder cooperative relationships between agencies. Competition for government and nongovernment funding and the natural tendency for non-profit agencies to fragment and go their separate ways raise some very important questions about the manner in which government funds might be administered to encourage comprehensive and integrated services in local communities.

Funding Sources and Agency Characteristics
The difficulty of categorizing the voluntary sector in terms of its activities has already been mentioned. It does not lend itself easily to classifications upon which statistical methods are based. Subject to this limitation, this section attempts to provide some background to the 133 agencies that were surveyed.[21]

The common thread among the agencies is that they received either grants or contracts or both from the provincial Ministry of Social Services. They all also provided services to families and children. The list generated by MSS, upon which the sample of 133 agencies is based, gives us some indication of the number of agencies that received government funding in each of the study areas.[22] Many more voluntary agencies in the metropolitan areas received funding than did those in non-metropolitan areas. It was pointed out earlier that in smaller communities, where there are limited numbers of agencies, it may be more difficult for government departments to request tenders for contracts. This result is congruent with other findings showing that voluntary agencies are unevenly distributed (Hatch 1981). Uneven distribution is considered to be one of the major weaknesses of relying on these agencies as instruments of social policy, since the impact of social policies will also be uneven.

Table 3.9 shows the age distribution of agencies, again categorized by whether they received provincial government grant funding only, contract funding only, or both grant and contract funding. The results show that the majority of the agencies in all three categories were founded between 1960 and 1970, confirming other findings that show the birth of many voluntary agencies during this period, in response to newly available federal and provincial government funding. Therefore, the government's policy shift to the purchase-of-service contracting model in the 1980s did not lead to a huge growth of new voluntary agencies. (There was an additional eighteen agencies founded in the 1980s amongst the 133 agencies surveyed.) What we have witnessed is a major expansion of the budgets of some of the existing voluntary agencies. The extent to which this policy shift has encouraged the growth of commercial provision can only be speculated upon.

Table 3.10 classifies the agencies by the size of their 1988-9 operating budgets.[23] The table confirms that agencies receiving only grant funding tended to have smaller annual budgets; 60 per cent of them operated on less than $150,000. When such agencies were located outside the large metropolitan areas, they tended to have smaller budgets than their urban counterparts. Agencies receiving contracts only were usually larger than those receiving grants only; 61 per cent had budgets over $500,000. Again, agencies in this category located in the large metropolitan communities were larger than their counterparts in medium and small-sized communities. Over 70 per cent had budgets over $500,000, compared to 50 per cent of the agencies located in medium and small-sized communities. Overall, the large metropolitan communities contained a higher proportion of larger agencies (annual operating budgets exceeding $1,000,000). Small and medium-sized communities contained a higher proportion of agencies with annual budgets between $500,000 and $1,000,000. These budgets included government and nongovernment funding.

Table 3.11 shows the different client groups targeted by agencies. The table includes all client groups of the agencies whether funded by

Table 3.9

Period agencies began operations, by community size

	Prior to 1959		1960-79		1980s		Total	
	No. of agencies	% of agencies	No. of agencies	% of agencies	No. of agencies	% of agencies	No. of agencies	% of agencies
Prov. grant only								
Overall	1	10.0	8	80.0	1	10.0	10	100.0
Large metropolitan communities	1	14.3	6	85.7	–	–	7	100.0
Small- and medium-sized communities	–	–	2	66.7	1	33.3	3	100.0
Prov. contract only								
Overall	6	13.6	33	75.0	5	11.4	44	100.0
Large metropolitan communities	4	16.7	16	66.6	4	16.7	24	100.0
Small- and medium-sized communities	2	10.0	17	85.0	1	5.0	20	100.0
Prov. grants and contracts								
Overall	8	18.6	33	76.8	2	4.7	43	100.0
Large metropolitan communities	4	15.4	21	80.8	1	3.8	26	100.0
Small- and medium-sized communities	4	23.5	12	70.6	1	5.9	17	100.0
Total								
Overall	15	15.5	74	76.3	8	8.2	97	100.0
Large metropolitan communities	9	15.8	43	75.4	5	8.8	57	100.0
Small- and medium-sized communities	6	15.0	31	77.2	3	7.5	40	100.0

Table 3.10

1988-9 Annual budget of non-profit agencies, by type of provincial funding and community size

	1988-9 Annual Budgets									
	<$150,000		>$150,000		>$500,000 <$1,000,000		<1,000,000		Total	
	No. of agencies	% of agencies	No. of agencies	% of agencies	No. of agencies	% of agencies	No. of agencies	% of agencies	No. of agencies	% of agencies
Grant funding only										
Overall	6	60.0	2	20.0	2	20.0	–	–	10	100.0
Large metropolitan communities	3	42.9	2	28.6	2	28.6	–	–	7	100.0
Small- and medium-sized communities	3	100.0	–	–	–	–	–	–	3	100.0
Contract funding only										
Overall	11	25.0	6	13.6	13	29.5	14	31.8	44	100.0
Large metropolitan communities	5	20.8	2	8.3	7	29.2	10	41.7	24	100.0
Small- and medium-sized communities	6	30.0	4	20.0	6	30.0	4	20.0	20	100.0

Grant and contract funding

Overall	5	11.6	12	27.9	11	25.6	15	34.9	43	100.0
Large metropolitan communities	2	7.7	8	30.8	3	11.5	13	50.0	26	100.0
Small- and medium-sized communities	3	17.6	4	23.5	8	47.1	2	11.8	17	100.0
Total										
Overall	22	27.7	20	20.6	26	26.8	29	29.9	97	100.0
Large metropolitan communities	10	17.5	12	21.1	12	21.1	23	40.4	57	100.0
Small-and medium-sized communities	12	30.0	8	20.0	14	35.0	6	15.0	40	100.0

Table 3.11

Client group targeted by agencies, by type of provincial funding (by number and percentage of agencies)

	Non-handicapped population only						Non-handicapped and handicapped population						Handicapped population only					
	Adults		Children		Both		Adults		Children		Both		Adults		Children		Both	
	No.	%	No.	%	No.	%	No.	%	No.	%	No.	%	No.	%	No.	%	No.	%
Grant funding only	2	20.0	3	30.0	5	50.0	–	–	–	–	–	–	–	–	–	–	–	–
Contract funding only	2	4.5	2	4.5	13	29.5	5	11.4	8	18.2	5	11.4	2	4.5	–	–	7	15.9
Grant and contract funding	1	2.3	3	4.7	17	39.5	7	16.3	2	4.7	6	13.9	1	2.3	–	–	6	13.9
Total	5	5.2	8	8.2	35	36.1	12	12.4	10	10.3	11	11.3	3	3.1	–	–	13	13.4

government or by the agencies' own fundraising activities. Forty-nine per cent of the agencies sampled provided services only to the non-handicapped population. Thirty-three of the agencies (34 per cent) provided services to both the non-handicapped and the handicapped populations. Another sixteen of the agencies (16.5 per cent) provided services exclusively to the handicapped population.[24]

Table 3.12 compares the proportion of income from different sources by the year in which the agency was founded. This table shows that agencies founded between 1980 and 1989 are the most dependent upon government funding, with 94.4 and 88.6 per cent of their total funding coming from government sources in 1982-3 and 1988-9 respectively. Provincial government contract funding made up the largest proportion of government-derived funds for these agencies, and this proportion increased in 1988-9. Agencies founded prior to 1959 also show an increase in the proportion of their income from government sources, and more specifically, from provincial government contracts in 1988-9. In contrast, agencies established in the 1960s and 1970s show a decline in the proportion of both contract and total funds received from government.

Disaggregating the different sources, the table shows that agencies founded between 1970 and 1979 received a higher proportion of provincial government grants than all other groups. As mentioned in Chapter 2, the expansion of Community Grants funding by the NDP government spawned many community-based groups, and these have continued to receive such funding for historical reasons. Nonetheless, this funding source declined from 20.6 per cent in 1982-3 to 13.4 per cent in 1988-9.

It is also interesting to note the changes in nongovernment sources of funding. Nongovernment funding constituted a higher proportion of total funding in 1982-3 (35.7 per cent) for agencies established prior to 1959 than for all other groups. This funding declined by 7 per cent in 1988-9, balancing a 7 per cent increase in government funding. Agencies established since the 1960s, however, increased their proportion of nongovernment funding in 1988-9.

When we disaggregate the nongovernment sources, the table shows some interesting trends. The proportion of United Way funding declined for all agencies except those established in the 1980s. The decrease is largest for agencies established prior to 1959, but this funding source continues to be higher for the older agencies than for agencies established later. Agencies that emerged in the 1980s in response to

Table 3.12

Percentage of different sources of funding for non-profit agencies, by period agencies began operations

	Before 1959 (15 agencies)		1960-9 (18 agencies)		1970-9 (56 agencies)		1980-9 (8 agencies)		Mid to late 1980s (19 agencies*)	
	1982-3	1988-9	1982-3	1988-9	1982-3	1988-9	1982-3	1988-9	1982-3	1988-9
All govt. sources	64.3	70.9	80.9	76.1	87.0	82.5	94.4	88.6	–	87.2
Prov. govt. grants	3.8	3.4	2.1	1.0	20.6	13.4	2.5	2.2	–	4.8
Prov. govt. contracts	53.8	61.8	71.9	69.5	60.4	59.4	75.8	83.2	–	79.8
Federal govt. funding	4.7	4.4	5.2	4.1	4.9	8.3	16.1	2.8	–	2.2
Municipal govt. funding	2.0	1.4	1.8	1.5	1.1	1.4	–	0.4	–	0.4
Nongovt. sources	35.7	29.0	19.1	23.9	13.0	17.5	5.5	11.4	–	12.8
United Way	5.6	3.7	2.0	1.5	1.4	1.4	0.5	2.2	–	1.2
Fee-for-service	6.9	7.5	10.7	8.5	2.5	3.5	2.2	4.2	·	2.6
Earned revenue	15.1	9.1	2.2	3.1	4.4	4.3	0.9	1.0	–	1.4
Own funding	7.5	7.8	2.9	7.9	4.1	7.0	0.6	3.7	–	7.0
Other	0.5	0.9	1.2	2.9	0.6	1.2	1.2	0.2	–	0.4

* These 19 agencies are not included in the total of 97. They are included to allow for comparisons with older established agencies.

contract funding are probably encouraged to apply for United Way funding, which carries more flexibility than other income sources. It appears that United Way funding is being re-allocated between old and new agencies.

All agencies demonstrated an increase in the proportion of income from their own fundraising efforts. The significant increases can be attributed to gaming activities (casinos and bingo), which have become important sources of revenue. Fee-for-service and other sources of earned revenue also represent important sources of non-government funding. Income from fee-for-service appears to have increased marginally for all agencies except those established between 1960 and 1969. Interestingly, the proportion of fee-for-service income is much higher for agencies established prior to the 1970s, when there was an expansion of provincial government funding for a wider range of services.

It seems that the older, established agencies are probably facing increased competition in their attempts to raise funding from non-government sources. While monies raised from their own fundraising increased for all agencies, the increase was only marginal for the older, established agencies. As mentioned, they also face competition for United Way funding. The decline in their nongovernment funding base has encouraged the older agencies to pursue contracts as a way of ensuring agency growth and survival. Newer agencies, on the other hand, have been seeking alternatives to contract funding in order to diversify their funding base. Diversification may make them less vulnerable to changes in the government policies but it also brings them into competition with agencies that have relied to a greater extent on non-government sources of finance.

Summary
Two sources of data on privatization are analyzed in the chapter. Government expenditure trends are based on published sources for the Ministry of Social Services, while the non-profit data are based on a province-wide survey of 133 agencies.

The data underscore an important development in the overall philosophy for the public sector. Instead of providing service it is to become an enabling authority, concerned mainly with contracting out services to third parties: non-profit, proprietary, and for-profit groups. The changed role demonstrates a clear separation between government funding and delivery, or administration, of those services.

A central theme in the chapter is exploration of the extent to which voluntary organizations can rely on philanthropy and charitable giving and still maintain their integral role in social service delivery. The available data suggest that private sources of income cannot replace government support of the sector, and that it is unrealistic to expect this sector to fill in the gaps should government reduce its funding. Voluntary agencies are unevenly distributed and more likely to be located in the major metropolitan areas, suggesting they are spread more thinly where need may be greatest. Purchase-of-service contracting not only influences how this sector relates to government, but also how agencies relate to one another as they compete for government and nongovernment sources of support.

4
The Evolving 'Partnership' between Government and the Voluntary Sector

The literature gives many reasons for the popularity of contracting out to non-profit agencies. Particular administrations have given different weight to different reasons, depending on ideology. Governments have recognized that it is easier for non-profit agencies to mount programs to meet new and emerging needs than for government departments to do so. It is also easier to change program direction or to cut back on services when they are delivered by non-profit organizations. As well, contracting enables the government to implement programs from which it wishes to distance itself politically, even as it takes advantage of the already established credibility of non-profit organizations for program initiative. Further, contracting encourages decentralization and a participatory democracy at the local level.

The purpose of this chapter is to assess whether contracting between government and the voluntary sector follows the competitive market model. It also sets out to assess the methods used to secure the accountability of voluntary agencies that contract with specific government departments for service delivery. We have seen that the transformation of this sector into a major provider of social services has been accompanied by greater dependence upon contract funds. Reliance on public funds implies that voluntary agencies will be subject to some degree of government control. Understanding current methods for ensuring accountability should provide the groundwork to predict likely developments and their impact on the sector. The analysis is based on quantitative and qualitative information provided by the executive directors of the 133 agencies surveyed.

A Competitive Market Model?
The case for privatization rests on the efficiency-economy-choice argument, which appeals to those who believe that public provision and

waste are inseparable. Government provision is said to be wasteful because public employees are not faced with the same constraints as private sector employees to provide an efficient service. Purchase-of-service contracting is considered more efficient because it is seen as encouraging voluntary and other organizations to act as firms in competing for contracts.

Few studies compare the productivity of public and private provision of social services. This is not surprising when one considers the difficulty of measuring outcome and arriving at a cost-per-unit measure. Studies demonstrating cost savings to government through contracting have concentrated on areas other than social service provision, such as refuse collection, electricity, or water supply. Kitchen (1976) showed for example that contracted-out services in Surrey, British Columbia, were 18 per cent cheaper per household than municipal services in Burnaby, British Columbia. McDavid's study (1984) of Canadian cities with a population over 10,000 showed that in 1980, municipal collection was 50.9 per cent more expensive per household than private collection ($42.29 vs. $28.03). Similar results were demonstrated in a study by McAfee and McMillan (1986).

Contracting is a strategy used by government to encourage competition for contracts, and the contract is supposedly awarded to the lowest bidder complying with the advertised requirements of a service. Competition leads to greater cost-effectiveness because the true cost of providing services is revealed in the bidding process. Contracts are awarded to those offering the best quality service for the least cost (DeHoog 1984). Through monetary incentive and the threat of not renewing contracts, the government ensures that the service provider is efficient and responsive to consumer needs. The process of awarding contracts is therefore of vital importance.

Table 4.1 shows, however, that tendering is not the predominant method by which agencies are awarded contracts. The data are based on a multiple response question which recognized that agencies may have several contracts and be able to respond positively on all the listed procurement methods. In other words, instead of being asked on a contract-by-contract basis how each contract administered by their organizations was procured, agency executive directors answered whether any of the procurement methods listed applied to any of the contracts awarded to their organizations. The table therefore presents data on the agency level, showing the agency perspective on the methods by which they were most likely to be awarded contracts.

Table 4.1

Method by which non-profit agencies were awarded contracts

Method of contract award	Overall sample		Lower Mainland and Victoria		Region outside the Lower Mainland and Victoria	
	No. of agencies	% of agencies	No. of agencies	% of agencies	No. of agencies	% of agencies
Tender for contracts	63	47.3	42	52.5	21	39.6
Respond to official advertisements	42	31.6	25	31.3	17	32.1
Contracted and asked if interested	76	57.1	48	60.0	28	52.8
Given a direct offer	83	62.4	48	60.0	35	66.0
Other means*	56	42.1	34	42.5	22	41.5

* Includes writing proposals, approaching the ministry.

Table 4.1 shows that 62.4 per cent of the agencies were given a direct offer on at least one contract. Another 57.1 per cent mentioned that they were approached by the ministry and asked if they were interested in providing a particular service. It is not clear whether the agencies approached were then invited to make a competitive bid. The table also shows that there was little regional variation in the way that agencies procured contracts. Direct offer seems to have been the most prevalent method, even though the nature of the data leaves this more as an impression than as a statistical conclusion based on the number of contracts. Executive directors had various comments to make about direct offers:

We apply every year and get our contracts renewed.

We were given a direct offer and never had to tender. Usually the grant giving body comes to us to request a renewal. Our contracts have been automatically renewed every year since 1982. Even when there is a direct offer government implies that somehow there has been a tendering process. We know that they have a list of potential bidders. We're always worried that someone out there will do it cheaper and will take this service away from us.

Most executive directors interpreted automatic renewal as a sign that their agencies were providing a service that was satisfactory to government. It appears that services are most likely to be tendered when they are new, or if a current contract is being terminated. Even then, however, executive directors indicated that the rules on tendering are not clear:

Tenders are not always publicized. There are no defined process or set criteria for tendering. This vagueness allows MSS to approach as many or as few agencies as it wants. MSS uses tendering as a smokescreen to award contracts to whomever it chooses.

Contracts are not awarded on merit. We know some agencies are given contracts when they don't have the capability of carrying it through. They have no track record. They are given contracts because they are prepared to bid cheap.

The calibre of the tender proposal has no influence on how MSS selects a provider.

Out-of-town contractors are winning contracts to provide services here locally. This takes away programs from our agency. However, this government [Social Credit] is only interested in competition and saving money.

Government's tendering process and procedures are not clear. They have no idea what programs they want and the objectives are not always clear. They are unclear what and how a new program should look like. This vagueness allows government to make political decisions regarding who they want as a contractor.

In spite of its limitations, Table 4.1 clearly reveals that the contracting process is far more complicated than open, competitive bidding in which the contract is awarded to the lowest complying bidder. In many instances, the various government departments may have their choice limited to a small number of agencies that have developed the expertise and facility to provide a particular service. The executive directors seemed to be suggesting that the rules were fuzzy and that contracts are not necessarily awarded to those with the appropriate expertise. It is possible that the government's interest is to spread the work around. Concentrating services as well as dollars in one or two societies may create a kind of monopoly the government may have wished to avoid.

When an agency is already providing a service, it is usually renewed on a yearly basis. The agency may have acquired that service through a tender, but the contract is invariably renewed if the agency performs satisfactorily. Contracting agencies are difficult to replace, especially if they have developed service expertise over time. Changing contractors from year to year would be disruptive to clients, and newer agencies would require high start-up costs. Most executive directors interpreted this seemingly automatic yearly renewal as a direct offer. Thus, instead of the market model – in which government and non-profit agencies see themselves as independent buyers and sellers of service – there exists a situation of mutual dependency. The non-profit agencies have the expertise, staff, and facility to deliver services, while government is in the position of authority and is responsible for services.

The failure of the contracting process to follow the competitive market model contradicts the rationale behind the government's privatization strategy, the intent of which was to make services more cost effective. Brenton (1985) claims that those who support an expanded role for the voluntary sector are often persuaded by claims that the sector can provide services more cheaply and therefore more cost effectively. Evidence supporting this claim is inconclusive. The small number of studies that have attempted to compare the costs of government and voluntary sector provision have raised questions about methodology. Did researchers compare like with like? Did they pay adequate attention to different rates of pay, standards, and service effectiveness in the two sectors? Brenton also points out that confused terminology can also perpetuate the myth of cost effectiveness, 'where the distinction between voluntary organizations and volunteers, and between those voluntary bodies which employ paid staff and those which rely on unpaid labour, are blurred' (1985:110). Evidence of cost effectiveness was strongest where volunteers were used most extensively and where the organizations were small and not unionized. Both Hatch (1981) and Wolfenden (1978) show that as voluntary agencies became more established and institutionalized, or employed paid staff, their costs approximated those of the public sector.

The above evidence suggests that government may save costs by delegating a major service providing role to the voluntary sector if volunteers substitute for paid workers or voluntary agencies employ lower paid, non-unionized labour. Since governments everywhere are under pressure to reduce social spending, the devolution of service delivery to the voluntary sector in the name of pluralism and empowerment may furnish an environment in which volunteers and lower paid workers gradually substitute for trained professionals. The Korbin Report (1993) estimated that the contracted community social service sector employs 30,000 people, with 20,000 employed directly on provincial social service contracts. Seventy-five per cent of workers are female and 44 per cent work part-time. A survey of 494 organizations receiving $100,000 or more showed that 26 per cent of the agencies were represented by a union, making up almost half the workforce in these agencies. There are wage inequities throughout the sector,[1] raising questions about the standard and level of service provided.

Accountability and Regulation of the Voluntary Sector
The relationship between government and the voluntary sector is often discussed within the context of accountability, a concept that means different things to different people. The use of this term needs to be clarified if any analysis of the relationship is to be fruitful. When applied to bureaucratic structures, the term 'accountability' refers to the ways and means by which control is exercised over those to whom

power is delegated (Smith and Hague 1971). The line of accountability within government bureaucracy can generally be traced through each level of executive authority to the next. The levels of executive authority are ultimately accountable to the legislature, 'which is assisted in its surveillance of expenditures by an independent audit agency' (Smith 1971:27). Members of the legislature owe their position to democratic election in which all adults can participate. Accountability, in a political sense, is established through the machinery of representative democracy, which is reasonably well understood.

Voluntary organizations, on the other hand, are not legitimized through either democratic process or wide public participation. Although they provide a structure through which citizens can become involved in self-help, communal effort, and altruistic expression, their legitimacy is limited to small interest groups and small specific constituencies on whose behalf they claim to act. Even within these limited constituencies the extent of public participation is not always clear. This does not necessarily negate questions about the accountability of this sector, but it does point to the complicated nature of the topic.

When government uses nongovernmental social institutions, such as voluntary organizations and universities, as instruments to carry out its ends, the concept of accountability becomes much more elusive. It becomes entangled with issues of the effectiveness of these agencies and the desirability of the objectives they pursue. Robinson (1971) suggests that it is important to distinguish between three types of accountability when government departments contract with nongovernment institutions: program, process, and fiscal responsibility.

Program accountability is used to judge whether the contractor has successfully fulfilled the goals set out in a contract or project. The concept implies that the final product can be described in detail and that the fund provider has clear standards to evaluate the contractor's performance. Robinson (1971) argues that even when the fund provider and the contractor have similar and compatible goals, however, it is difficult to assess the quality of work performed because of differences in professional judgment. When it is not possible to define goals as clearly, the issue becomes more complex. Whereas it is easy to specify standards in road construction, for example, it is much more difficult to specify the outcome of a program for children who come into care. It is therefore easier to measure whether certain processes have been carried out. Thus, in measuring process accountability, the contract may focus on the number of staff working full-time, staff qualification, the staff-client ratio, the physical plant, and so on. Fiscal responsibility concerns expenditure made according to the terms designated by the contract. The contracting agency is expected to maintain proper accounting records. The concern of the fund provider – the government – is to determine 'whether the tax payer has received adequate returns for the funds invested' (Robinson 1971:103).

Delegating the service delivery role to third parties implies that control can be exercised indirectly through the disbursement of finance. It is therefore important to establish how public authorities will ensure that the public continues to enjoy the protections of statutory services of an agreed-upon quality. When government involvement is limited to contract management, the accountability and effectiveness of third-party organizations are particularly important, especially as it is not always clear that these organizations allocate their energies and resources 'in accordance with some abstract criteria of need or equity' (Wolfenden Committee 1978:58). Voluntary organizations have traditionally made their services available on the basis of charity rather than as a matter of the statutory rights of the clients. Contracting out has also highlighted the discontinuities characteristic of the human services – discontinuities that are perhaps not so apparent when these services are provided through government offices which automatically put in place government procedures and regulations, however imperfect.

Accountability and regulation are also important in light of an uncertain government policy toward for-profit sector competition in the social services. Competition for government funding against a background of restraint has led to tactical debates over standards or quality of service. There are those who would like to see Canada's federal legislative framework changed to allow subsidies only for non-profit organizations.[2] Krashinsky (1986) argues, however, that the for-profit/non-profit debate is less relevant than the need for appropriate government regulation and monitoring to ensure that all agencies deliver quality service on the government's behalf.

The following sections examine the mechanisms used by government departments to ensure greater accountability of non-profit agencies delivering services in British Columbia. Two caveats apply to any attempt at generalization. The first is that the contracting-out experiences of different types of non-profit organizations are likely to vary according to their historical dependence on government funding and to whether this funding was initially received with strings attached. The second is that agencies initially founded to meet neighbourhood or community needs are likely to have a substantially different approach to contracting from that of agencies founded in response to available government funding.

This discussion highlights some of the difficulties in the contracting process. This is not to say that non-profit agencies and government officials invariably experience conflict or difficulties, or that tensions cannot be overcome. Tensions are most likely to arise when the two parties interpret the objectives of a funded service differently. There is more scope for disagreement when the objectives are not clearly defined, or when one party wishes to change the direction of a particular service in a way that is not agreeable to the other. The scope of the discussion is perhaps better understood if one places non-profit agencies on a continuum: at one end they are most like volunteer associations, and at the other, they were founded or have evolved in response to government funding availability. Agencies that least resemble government, or resemble volunteer-based organizations most, are more likely to experience conflict.

Standards

When the 133 executive directors of the surveyed agencies were asked if their contracts with different provincial government departments contained written standards of service, sixty-three (47.4 per cent) replied 'yes,' sixty-nine (51.9 per cent) replied 'no,' and one (0.8 per cent) replied 'don't know.' Generally, there seemed to be some confusion over standards, stemming from process and program accountability. Because it is difficult to arrive at agreed-upon outcome measures, executive directors often mentioned that their agency had developed policy and procedure manuals and that these set the standards for their agencies. There was a mix of responses to the question about standards:

The society has a body of policies and guidelines developed over the years. These policies and procedures are updated annually. Our various programs also maintain standards relative to their particular area of concern. For example, the lay counselling program speaks to needs and limitations of volunteers, training, levels of competence, legal considerations, confidentiality of clients, reporting procedures, and so on.

We can't say we set standards. We have professional staff who belong to associations that set standards. In an informal way we do meet with other societies, like ours, to discuss standards.

Our contracts contain standards that deal with quantity of service but not quality. We're told how many clients we're supposed to see. Nothing in the contract tells us about procedures, and what to do to get a desired result.

We're flying by the seat of our pants. We started in 1986 and are still very new. As we evolve we will clarify and identify these standards. A lot of operational and standard issues are learnt as the employee delivers services.

There are no universal standards. Standards for each service depend on the proposals written and the expertise of the personnel in that service area and geographical region. This begs the whole issue of service quality and service standards and whether services in each region meet the same standards. Apart from licensing requirements there are no standards.

Other executive directors mentioned that they were affiliated to national or provincial bodies that set guidelines to which their agency adhered:

Our standards are adopted from the Federation of Private Child Agencies of BC standard guidelines. This is restricted to agencies providing residential care for children using a 'staffed' model.

We are currently developing policies and procedures to comply with the standards of the Council on Accreditation of Services for Families and Children. We will apply to become an accredited organization.

Executive directors pointed out that government appeared to be more interested in balancing budgets than in ensuring that voluntary agencies provided quality service:

Government is out to get cheap contracts. Standards are not important. It seems that it is up to the agencies to get as much as they can. Government tries to get you to do as much as you can for as cheaply as possible. If standards had to be written down, government will be forced to pay for these.

The ministries are concerned with how much service they can get for the money specified in the contract. They don't bother about quality. They know that we'll worry about that.

We are doing more with less money. We can no longer maintain the standards of our services in the way that we had originally written [in] the contract when government was funding us more appropriately. The system seems to have evolved into a numbers game wherein everyone loses. There is less of a desire to help others than in maintaining job tenure or ensuring that the contract goes to the lowest bidder.

Government gains through tendering because they do not have to put out the dollars. It means that they can pay only for service delivery, but not for systems and other things that go with accountability, such as trained staff, training, professional development, monitoring and so on. Supervision is not taken into account and not paid for; so there are no checks. Females end up in non-profit sector jobs where there is little money.

There also appeared to be different experiences depending on the ministry, or branch, through which the contract was obtained:

With Mental Health every item is laid out in great detail and we have a tremendous amount of paperwork even for a $5,000 contract.

We have a good working relationship with the Attorney General. They give us a lot of freedom regarding how we use their money. We have some scope in incorporating our ideas and processes.

[The Ministry of] Health is obsessed with quality assurance. We would like to have flexibility and looser guidelines but we recognize that this could be abused by other non-profit organizations.

With MSS, expectations are informally discussed.

MSS is very specific about what they want you to do. Recently they have included staff qualification requirements when they were tendering on a contract on professional counselling.

MSS gives us free rein to develop services and programs as we see fit.

When those who responded positively to whether contracts contained written standards of service were asked to specify what the standards were, they invariably referred to process elements such as staff qualification, staff-client ratio, and so on. In some cases contracts specified process measures; in others the agency specified them in its submission. These submissions then became the basis for contract negotiations and service development and delivery. Again there appeared to be great variation depending on the ministry, the contract, and the issues:

> The guidelines range from contract to contract and issue to issue, from very specific detailed requirements to vague ambiguous requirements. Much of the schedule of service language, in most of our contracts, is based on our proposals. We specify staff qualifications, staff/client ratios and so on.

> In two cases we inherited programs from government services; some issues are addressed simply by historical procedures; some issues are addressed simply by holding us to the terms of our initial proposal.

> We have to send proof of staff qualifications to the licensing board. MSS contracts do not specify staff qualifications whereas [Ministry of] Health contracts do.

> Qualification and staff ratios have to be left to the agency. If we wrote these down and agreed upon it MSS would have to increase its funding.

> These [standards of service] are not contained in the contract. MSS relies on the integrity of non-profits to hire qualified staff if they say they will.

> Contracts state that staff must have sufficient skills and qualification to deliver services to clients. Our staffing parallels ministry employee classifications.

Those interviewed mentioned that both staff qualification and the numbers of staff hired depended very much on what government was willing to pay. Without sufficient funds these agencies were sometimes forced to hire less qualified staff or to hire fewer highly qualified staff. The problem is even more acute in the non-metropolitan areas, where these employers experience difficulty in recruiting and retaining suitably qualified staff:

We know better than to ask for more money. Salaries are too low and people with qualifications aren't going into the field.

We had a 130 per cent turnover in staff last year because of poor salaries. People with qualification will join us just to get their foot in the door and then they're gone. There is a lot of time spent in hiring and retraining.

Being in the north we can't always find suitably trained people for the job. So we hire people who have personal suitability but we need money to upgrade their education and qualification on the job. The ministries are adamant that they do not provide money for professional development.

We have some problems with this ministry's [MSS] attitude. They won't contract with us if we pay our staff the government rate. Does this mean that they want less qualified staff to deliver services? They are contracting with us because we pay lower wages to our employees and this saves the government money. They are so concerned with balancing budgets and not at all concerned with effectiveness.

The survey data indicated that the voluntary agencies surveyed were not always in agreement whether contracts should contain explicit guidelines. Some agencies wanted more specific guidelines, but others saw such rules and regulations as undue interference with the internal business of the agency:

We have full say over our programs. We can't have government dictating to us.

These are our employees. The Ministry [MSS] cannot tell us what to do. We retain the right to hire and keep who we will.

We would like guidelines on staff qualification, staff client ratios and so on. We would like these to be written in the contract so we can budget better.

We don't want or need more guidelines. We will be accountable but we do not want interference in how we provide services.

We don't want to write in too specific standards because the government obliges you to follow them.

We want more guidelines with respect to qualification, criminal checks, liability issues. We want government's input but they are happy that we define these for ourselves.

Because they're hiring us as an agency and purchasing our services, it is our responsibility to establish guidelines. Government should check these out before they purchase our services.

We would prefer something about staff qualification in our contracts. This would raise the consciousness of the management [of non-profit organizations] about professional development. Most non-profits have wonderful intentions but they have little business sense and don't value their human resources.

In addition to the open-ended questions on standards, executive directors of the surveyed agencies were asked if contracts with the different ministries contained guidelines on a number of process features shown in Table 4.2. This table shows that more than 50 per cent of the agencies that received funding from the respective ministries said that their contracts did not contain any of the listed guidelines. The exceptions are qualification of staff when contracting with the Ministry of Health (59.3 per cent said 'yes'), and criminal checks on staff (71 per cent of agencies contracting with MSS and 77.4 per cent contracting with Attorney General said 'yes').

Executive directors were also asked to indicate how and whether guidelines on qualification of staff and staff-client ratio were specified in their contracts. Table 4.3 shows that ninety-five of the agencies (71.4 per cent) said that qualification of staff was left up to the agency. One hundred and ten agencies (82.7 per cent) said that the staff-client ratio was negotiated during the contracting process, while eighty-one (60.9 per cent) said that the staff-client ratio was left up to the agency. Again, these were multiple response questions, suggesting that agencies had that experience with at least one contract.

Executive directors mentioned that although district supervisors in MSS offices recognized the problems faced by agencies, their hands were tied because expenditure guidelines were usually imposed centrally by the Department of Finance in Victoria. Executive directors felt that they

Table 4.2

Number and percentage of non-profit agencies that received ministry guidelines on the selected process features

	Process feature												
Ministry awarding contract	Qualification of staff		Staff/Client ratio		Residential facility regulation		Client expenses		Criminal record checks		Emergency procedures	
	No.	%	No.	%	No.	%	No.	%	No.	%	No.	%
MSS (107 agencies)	44	41.1	46	43.8	25	23.4	34	31.8	76	71.0	33	30.8
Health (54 agencies)	32	59.3	20	37.0	15	27.8	10	18.5	17	31.5	15	27.8
AG (31 agencies)	7	22.6	11	35.5	8	25.8	6	19.4	24	77.4	10	32.3
Mental Health* (19 agencies)	8	42.1	8	42.1	2	10.5	4	21.1	8	42.1	2	10.5

* Mental Health Services is a branch in the Ministry of Health. The 19 agencies are included in the number shown contracting with the Ministry of Health.

had only one real opportunity for contract negotiations – when their agencies first set up a service. The initial negotiation on many of the listed issues set the baseline for the future. In other words, subsequent renewals of a contract tend to be based on renegotiating some of the terms agreed upon in the initial agreement. Usually, agencies were given the amount by which the budget could be expanded but conditions discussed in the initial setting up of the service were taken for granted, as summed up by the following comments:

> We submit a budget for the following year for renewal purposes. Government counters and if we don't agree, they cut off our money.

> Renegotiating is redundant – they just give us the stipulated increase.

> Our contract went to tender because we wanted more money. We were not prepared to provide the same level of service for the money they gave us. MSS is too cheap.

Table 4.3

How guidelines for qualification of staff and staff/client ratio were specified in the contracts

	Qualification of staff		Staff/Client ratio	
	No.	%	No.	%
Written and defined in the contract	49	36.8	40	30.1
Implied (oral)	41	30.8	26	19.5
Negotiated through contract (addendum)	9	6.8	110	82.7
Left to the agency	95	71.4	81	60.9
Licensing	14	10.5	6	4.5
Written in the proposal	3	2.3	3	2.3

Executive directors of the surveyed agencies were also asked if their agencies had internal standards for service; 125 agencies (94 per cent) answered 'yes' and eight (6 per cent) answered 'no.'[3] When asked to specify what the standards were, executive directors referred to their policy manuals, which covered the checklist shown in Table 4.4.

Monitoring

Table 4.5 shows that the majority of agencies contracting with each of the listed ministries (more than 60 per cent) mentioned some form of

Table 4.4

Number and percentage of non-profit agencies having internal standards for the listed features

	Yes		No		Don't Know	
	No.	%	No.	%	No.	%
Hours of work	127	95.5	5	3.8	1	0.8
Wages and conditions of employment	127	95.5	5	3.8	1	0.8
Client confidentiality	124	93.2	8	6.0	1	0.8
Benefits	119	89.5	13	9.8	1	0.8
Employee development	115	86.5	17	12.8	1	0.8
Safety and health	107	80.5	24	18.0	2	1.5
Grievance procedures	108	81.2	24	18.0	1	0.8
Board evaluation procedures	94	70.7	38	28.6	1	0.8

monitoring, either informal, formal, or through committee reviews. The Ministry of Health and its Mental Health Branch appear to have done the most monitoring. The table provides no indication of the volume of contracts by ministry per agency. It is thus entirely possible that the 61.7 per cent of agencies that contracted with MSS and also indicated some form of monitoring represented the bulk of contracts with this ministry. The responses of the executive directors indicated great variability in how agencies were being monitored. The overall impression is that agencies were not usually clear about the issues around which they might be monitored:

All we have to do is send in a glowing report. They have never checked anything or how things are done.

All MSS goes on is the report we send in rather than an intimate knowledge of our agency or our services.

There is no long term view. There exists a wide variety of contracts with a lack of common standards leading to multiplicity of service quality. More monitoring and certification are needed.

The ministry does not come around and check enough. The field social worker is finding it difficult to meet her monitoring responsibility as she has too many contracting agencies. Eight months into our contracts and we discovered that we were supposed to meet with the liaison worker.

We have a liaison worker and a social worker for each person in our home and we have very regular contact. The ministry liaison worker attends our staff meetings and gets feedback from the clients through the social worker who refers clients.

There is no assessment, no monitoring and no interest in how we are doing. Monitoring, evaluation and standards should be clearly laid out because without these, we non-profits can do anything we like and we are not accountable. Government is concerned with financial accountability. There should be more controls.

The ministry doesn't question anything. We could get away with doing almost nothing. Our board of directors is supposed to monitor but the contract mentions nothing about this. I wonder how many people sitting on these boards of directors realize that they're liable.

This informal monitoring is very effective. It is astonishing how Corrections [a branch within the attorney general's ministry] knows what is happening here all the time. Our clients are their clients. Their staff can figure out a lot of things just by talking to our staff and the clients who they have referred. This gossipy informal intelligence keeps people on their toes.

Government ministries should build into contracts quality analysis, such as client satisfaction questions. This way MSS will have an objective way of evaluating the service.

It appears that the nature of monitoring is largely determined by the working relationship between agencies and government departments. The tone of that relationship, in turn, is set by the negotiations preceding the contract. The negotiations provide the opportunity for government officials and the contracting agency to articulate their expectations with regard to the budget, service standards, if any, and other issues. Negotiations over these issues can then set the tone of the working relationship between the two parties. This working relationship can also influence the outcome of subsequent renewals as well as

Table 4.5

Method by which ministries monitored their guidelines

	Informal only		Formal only		Through committee reviews only		Formal, informal, and through committee reviews		Total	
	No. of agencies	% of agencies	No. of agencies	% of agencies	No. of agencies	% of agencies	No. of agencies	% of agencies	No. of agencies	% of agencies
MSS (107 agencies)	12	11.2	31	29.0	2	1.9	21	19.6	66	61.7
Health (54 agencies)	11	20.4	21	38.9	1	1.9	9	16.7	42	77.8
AG (31 agencies)	5	16.1	11	35.5	1	3.2	4	12.9	21	67.7
Mental Health (19 agencies*)	4	19.0	11	57.9	–	–	11	57.9	16	84.2

* These agencies are included in the number listed as contracting with the Ministry of Health.

the acquisition of new service contracts. The importance of the working relationship between the fund provider and the contracting agency cannot be overstated.

For the organizations surveyed, the working relationship was likely to be smooth, comfortable, and based on mutual understanding if the executive director was familiar with the culture of the public sector. This situation was most frequent when the executive director was a former employee of government, or had a track record of working with different ministries. These executive directors were usually aware that conflict may arise from different interpretations of the objectives of a project. They pointed out that it was important for executive directors to understand the conditions under which they were committing their agencies to a service. Some executive directors fully embraced the notion that in undertaking to deliver services under contract they agreed with government policy. Others saw contracting as important for the growth and viability of their society, but saw it as important that they influence government in the negotiation process using orthodox means of influence. They may, for example, push for the extension of boundaries defining who is eligible for service. Or, in the event of a disagreement, they may inform the local official that they are prepared to resort to more radical measures once they have exhausted all the orthodox means.

On the other hand, smaller or newer agencies with executive directors who were less familiar with how government works were more likely to experience some difficulty. Conflict between the two parties usually centred on a difference in the terms of reference contained in their contracts or on the agency's policies for client selection and service delivery. The government mandate may be to fund treatment services, while many voluntary agencies see a greater need for preventative services. The executive directors of these agencies may be more ready to resort to the more extreme means of influence earlier in the confrontation. For example, they may approach the media, the local member of the legislative assembly (MLA), or even send a delegate to the provincial government. Other societies may experience conflict and may not have any contact at all with government officials. The following remarks were typical expressions of conflict:

> They [government officials] have hired people without the appropriate qualifications. These people tell us who we should see, what we should do and how much service we should provide. They are involved and

concerned with short term solutions ... crisis-oriented as opposed to proactive.

We disagree on how money is spent and should be spent. We're not sure they know what the issues are. They don't trust us. They are concerned that we are too large and are going outside our mandate. We are spending a fair amount of time justifying our policies, procedures, staffing etc.

MSS contract goals for special needs are totally inappropriate. Our society wants to take in self referrals. MSS wants to do all the referrals.

MSS is trying to get our society to adhere to ministry policies and program. We no longer have control to set goals and to have open referrals in that our clients must go through MSS.

Other executive directors admitted that agency goals and government service requirements conflicted, but agreed that it was possible for them to attempt to change the terms of the contract to accommodate their agencies' goals. Still other agencies dealt with the problem by attempting to seek favour with government officials in the hope that this would lead to more contracts. These circumstances suggest that prospects for non-profit agencies contracting with government departments depend very much on the political savvy of their executive directors:

You can always tailor your proposals knowing what they have to offer. We went after the Family Initiatives money to pay for needed services. We used this money to supplement services which fitted in with our mandate and that met government's funding criteria.

We expanded our mandate to target those groups that were receiving government funding. We expanded and developed our resources for families and those who work with families.

Our agency used to focus on services to women. We had great funding problems. Now we provide services to women and children.

We changed our mandate to high risk/special needs from special needs because MSS tightened its mandate for funding.

We do not have an adversarial relationship. Instead we try to work creatively with the ministries to provide services to families and children.

When we contract we don't know what the client group will be. The ministry tells us during the tendering process what type of people they will be referring. It is impossible to plan long term.

The impression conveyed in the discussions with the executive directors was that contracting, as practiced in 1989, developed their grantsmanship to the point at which they became familiar with the culture, language and procedures of government. The executive directors felt that this skill enabled them to develop relationships with the funders that counteracted the power imbalance between government and the voluntary sector. Nevertheless, there was some question whether energy spent on such tactics might not be better spent developing efficient and responsible service delivery. As one executive director put it,

no one has the mandate to evaluate the quality of services. We need to set in place criteria for standards and evaluations. It is fine to have things out to tender but if there are no checks on services we're not doing the children in care, or those at risk of coming into care, any good. Instead of focusing on developing and delivering efficient and effective services, non-profit agencies worry whether they will still be in business should someone underbid them. There is no reason why contracts and standards cannot be standardized.

Reporting
Executive directors of the surveyed agencies were asked how often each of the ministries from which they received funding expected them to report on services and finances. This was a multiple response question, meaning that an agency with several contracts could have responded positively to several of the allotted categories of frequency at once. Agencies were classified by whether they provided residential services only, non-residential services only, both residential and non-residential services, or were not involved in direct service provision. The data were incorporated into Table 4.6.

The table reveals that residential services required more frequent reporting than non-residential services. This is to be expected given that

Table 4.6

Mean score of service reporting requirements for non-profit agencies

Type of service	MSS	Health	AG	Mental Health	Other prov. govt. dept.	Municipal govt.	Federal govt.	United Way
Residential services only	7.1	5.7	12.2	–	–	0.5	3.0	4.0
Non-residential services only	5.3	4.6	7.7	6.6	9.0	1.5	6.1	0.9
Residential and non-residential services	6.9	6.7	6.3	5.9	5.3	2.2	4.9	0.8
Not in direct service*	1.0	4.0	–	–	–	–	–	–
Overall	5.9	5.5	7.6	6.2	7.1	1.8	5.5	1.0

* One umbrella organization was not in direct service delivery.
Note: Responses were scored in the following way: report more than once a month (18); report once per month (12); report once per quarter (4); report once a year (1); report less than once a year (.5). A mean score was then calculated for non-profit organizations contracting with each funding agency or department. Therefore, the higher the score, the greater is the frequency of reporting.

residential services cater to the more vulnerable client groups (i.e., children in care). It is not clear, however, why municipalities and the federal government appear to be exceptions to the rule in this category. It could be that they provide a smaller portion of the funding for such services and therefore do not require such frequent reporting. Reporting frequencies for agencies providing both residential and non-residential services are higher than for agencies providing non-residential services only. Scoring on residential services may shift the scores higher. Overall, the Ministry of the Attorney General requires agencies to report most frequently (7.6), followed by other provincial ministries (7.1), and then Mental Health (6.2). Reporting frequencies required by MSS, the Ministry of Health, and the federal government are higher than those required by the municipal government and the United Way. The impression gained from the interviews is that reporting tends to be more frequent when a government department has recently begun to contract out services, possibly explaining the high score for the other provincial government ministries.

Table 4.7 uses the same scoring system as Table 4.6 to demonstrate the frequency with which agencies report on finances by type of service provided. The table shows that most government ministries require financial reports approximately every quarter. The municipal government and United Way require such reports approximately annually. There do not appear to be any differences in financial reporting requirements between residential and non-residential services. The data are limited because they do not reflect that reporting may be related to the size of contracts, i.e., the larger the contracts, the more frequent the reporting requirement. Because the data were not collected contract by contract, it is not possible to provide that level of analysis.

Again the variability described by the executive directors of these agencies is quite striking. Some executive directors maintained that no reports were requested, even on the number of clients served. Others indicated that government departments were moving beyond financial accountability and attempting to establish other sorts of controls. Yet others indicated that they had tightened up their own internal reporting and evaluation procedures because of agency concerns about accountability and the seeming disinterest of government ministries over this issue:

We didn't even have to report on the numbers of clients served. There is a complete lack of accountability.

Table 4.7

Mean score of financial reporting requirements for non-profit agencies

Type of service	MSS	Health	AG	Mental Health	Other prov. govt. dept.	Municipal govt.	Federal govt.	United Way
Residential services only	1.5	3.0	5.7	–	–	1.0	3.0	4.0
Non-residential services only	2.0	3.1	3.4	3.2	6.0	1.5	4.8	1.2
Residential and non-residential	3.6	4.6	4.2	3.1	5.4	1.3	5.0	0.9
Not in service provision*	1.0	4.0	–	–	–	–	–	–
Overall	2.5	3.7	3.9	3.1	5.6	1.4	4.8	1.1

* One umbrella organization was not in direct service delivery.

Note: Responses were scored in the following way: report more than once a month (18); report once per month (12); report once per quarter (4); report once a year (1); report less than once a year (.5). A mean score was then calculated for non-profit organizations contracting with each funding agency or department. Therefore, the higher the score, the greater is the frequency of reporting.

Contracting has forced us to look at our own assessment and evaluation tools. We have our own evaluation procedures that we submit to
MSS regularly, but they are only interested in financial accountability.

Regulation and control are increasing. We now have a liaison worker
and a social worker for each person in our homes.

In the past MSS was concerned only with financial accountability. Now
their workers are showing more interest in the services and are starting
to develop closer working relationships with voluntary agencies. This
can create some problems because they may want us to do things that
may not be agreeable to our agency.

Client Selection

Executive directors of the surveyed non-profit agencies pointed out that
government stipulated more stringent eligibility criteria for clients to
receive services from non-profit agencies under contract to government. Social workers in MSS act as gatekeepers to these services. This
role became formalized during the restraint period and less flexibility
was given to contracting agencies to accept clients on open referrals.
Under contract funding, an agency agrees to provide services to clients
referred by MSS workers. In essence then, non-profit agencies must
conform to government directives on services and client selection.

Although government has increasingly directed who should be
served under its contracted services, it has yet to provide directives on
staffing and program, as may be seen from Table 4.2. It nonetheless
influences staffing and services through its control over funding, showing that the independence of the non-profit sector may be illusory.
Again, the survey data convey the impression that the degree of flexibility exercised by voluntary agencies varies considerably:

The ministry effectively calls the shots even when they say they don't.
They tell us who can receive services, they refer the clients and tell us
how many clients we should be seeing. If they don't like our staff they
can cancel our contracts.

Our relationship is not arm's length. MSS screens and refers clients to
our services.

MSS doesn't really know what it wants. They define the client group
but they rely on us to develop services and programs as we see fit.

Our contracts are quite general. Each contract has appendices but these are not too specific.

Accountability and Partnership

It appears that the two sides of the contracting relationship wish to see themselves as independent buyers and sellers of services. Both try to minimize their mutual dependence, which they now refer to as a 'partnership,' by agreeing that the contractual relationship remain at 'arm's length.' The relationship was defined by one executive director as follows:

An arm's length relationship is one in which MSS defines their specific program needs and goals, and agrees to supply specified resources to the contractor to operate programs which address those needs and goals. MSS does not, however, control the day-to-day operations of the contractor as long as the services are provided as contracted. The contractors are not considered government employees and the contractor assumes all responsibility for hiring and supervision of staff.

In general, there is always some type of financial accountability attached to funding from all fund providers, and it does not seem to lead to contention between the two parties. The comments from the executive directors indicate that difficulties usually began from a perception that the funder sought control beyond requiring an accounting to show that money was spent as stipulated in the contract. Executive directors expressed different attitudes regarding this matter. At one end of the scale they took the view that contracts should clearly spell out staff qualification, staff-client ratios, monitoring, and evaluation tools used to ensure that voluntary agencies were accountable for producing a desired result. At the other end were those who viewed government-specified rules and regulations as undue meddling in the day-to-day operations of their agency.

Because contracts are defined as arm's length there appears to be a general agreement that the fund provider cannot interfere with the internal affairs of voluntary agencies. The data reviewed so far suggest that there is tremendous variation in government control from contract to contract, department to department, and issue to issue. It is not evident what leads government departments to exert greater control over hiring requirements. The impression from the interviews is that government is more likely to exert these controls where a service is therapeutic- or treatment-oriented, requiring specific skills or credentials for which the government is also prepared to pay. Some agencies expressed the desire for greater government control and seemed surprised that the only condition of their contracts was some form of financial accountability. Seen from the government's perspective, guidelines covering staffing, hours of work, and so on may seem like benevolent supervision, especially when an agency has asked for some guidance in its development as an agent of government. It is clear, however, that other agencies view this as undesirable interference. Agencies' lack of agreement over the types of control that are in their best interest is a matter for concern because it may create a climate in which too much control is exerted, endangering the effectiveness of the sector. One executive director described the dilemma facing voluntary organizations:

What is the happy medium between some government controls compared to a service that is totally community run? We need a benevolent dictator around quality – someone who can set standards for care without interfering with the agency's needs to be flexible so that we can guarantee quality care to clients. What we need are policies and procedures which allow fairness regardless of the whims and fancies of the district manager.

The question of effectiveness came up frequently in discussions with the executive directors. The term effectiveness is used interchangeably with accountability and means different things to different people. In the context of the voluntary sector, effectiveness is sometimes confused with the desirability of the activities and objectives of voluntary organizations. Issues associated with effectiveness are complex and only a brief summary can be presented here. Executive directors often discussed the following concerns about effectiveness: whether voluntary organizations were providing services that the community needed; whether agencies became self-perpetuating and sought funding to ensure their own survival instead of adapting to changing demands; whether they were cooperating and collaborating to avoid unnecessary duplication; whether services were being monitored and evaluated to ensure that the desired results were being achieved; and whether clients and members of voluntary agencies were satisfied with the work being done.

Apprehension was expressed that government departments were overly preoccupied with fiscal accountability and reports on the numbers of clients served. Monitoring and evaluation were regarded as inadequate. Executive directors also feared that government was contracting with agencies that could not provide adequate and effective services. The client was often forgotten as government tried to get as much for as cheaply as possible. Some executive directors were concerned that autonomy for voluntary organizations was often taken to mean that any person could set up an organization and provide services by any method it chose, regardless of what other individuals and organizations were doing. Implied in these discussions was the notion that voluntary organizations have to reconcile their freedom and autonomy not only with the measure of control that comes with external funding, but also with their responsibility to the community:

> We need to stop being seen as agencies who should be having bake sales, rummage sales etc., and that the job we're doing isn't considered worthy of regular and sustained government funding. We want and need more guidelines and there needs to be defined roles in the community as to who is responsible for what so that we avoid overlap and duplication of services. We don't have to be 'do-gooders' anymore. We need to define our identity, what we do and then be funded to do the job efficiently and effectively. This would eliminate empire building, competition, back stabbing and non-cooperation between voluntary agencies.

> Accountability to the client is not built into the contracts. Can the client distinguish between peer counselling, registered counsellor, psychiatrist or psychologist? Counsellors don't have to be registered or licensed, so anybody can set themselves up as counsellors. We, as a professional non-profit agency, are resented by other non-profits who see us going after their sources of funding. They [non-profits in this locality] told me they won't refer to us.

The open-ended qualitative and quantifiable data indicate that the principal forms of accountability are fiscal and service reporting. Process accountability is left largely to the discretion of contracting officers in government departments and appears to be influenced by the relationship established between such officers and the contracting agency. Evaluation and monitoring of services, once the contract is signed, depend on staffing levels within government departments and the history of the working relationship between the two parties. The lack of a common monitoring framework has encouraged many voluntary agencies to establish their own evaluation and monitoring schemes. Program accountability appears to be intermittent.

It is obvious that the funding relationship casts its shadow over all dealings between the two sectors. Funding through contracting has given voluntary agencies a new lease on life and an important role in service delivery. It has also imposed a relationship in which the power is all on one side – if only funding is considered. The two parties are mutually dependent, however, in the sense that government depends on agencies that have developed the expertise and resources for service delivery to clients who have a statutory right to those services. Fund providers need to understand the purposes and motives of voluntary organizations. They must also balance their need for control and accountability with support for the sector's freedom and autonomy if they are to avoid endangering its effectiveness. The responsibility for fostering a positive working relationship does not lie solely with fund providers. Voluntary organizations must recognize that public funders have to answer to specific constituents. They must also demonstrate their effectiveness and responsibility to both their funders and their community.

Summary

Tendering is not the predominant method by which agencies are awarded contracts. Most of the non-profit agencies surveyed were given a direct offer on at least one contract. Another 60 per cent mentioned that they were approached and asked if they were interested in providing a particular service.

This chapter has examined several dimensions of the broad issue of accountability, raised by the financial relationship between government and the voluntary sector. The involvement of non-profit societies in service provision prompts an examination of how government safeguards the interests of the public, who are now entitled to such services.

The relationship between government and the voluntary sector is mediated through the contracting process, in which the interests, motives, and goals of the two sides are also articulated. The chapter suggests that the process can be fraught with difficulties. Government policies on contracting out lack a consistent and coherent framework. There is great variation within and between government departments, from contract to contract, and from issue to issue. Voluntary organizations also appear to be divided on issues. The government is attempting to increase the accountability of agencies by implementing more rigorous eligibility criteria for receiving government-subsidized services.

Accountability is inextricably linked to the concepts of effectiveness and responsibility. Fund providers and voluntary organizations need to agree on what constitutes fair practice, accountability, value for money, effectiveness, and methods of monitoring and evaluation that incorporate responsibility to the funder as well as to clients and the community. Greater control and accountability should not be implemented at the expense of flexibility that may contribute to the effectiveness of the voluntary sector. The sector must also take some initiative and responsibility for developing guidelines and approaches to accountability that will be in their best interest.

5
The Autonomy of the Voluntary Sector

The evidence presented in Chapter 3 indicates that the current expansion of the voluntary sector can be attributed to the growth of contract funding from the provincial government. The high proportion of government contract funds that they receive raises questions about the independence of these voluntary organizations. The goal of this chapter is to explore the ways in which government, through its control of funding, defines and shapes policies and practice within the voluntary sector. It also explores the strategies used by voluntary agencies to resist these pressures in order to maintain their autonomy.

The results presented in this text confirm research elsewhere (Urban Institute 1981) that voluntary organizations depend, to a large extent, on government sources of finance. Grants or contracts are usually given to an agency to enable it to pursue the statutory duties of the authorities, which they cannot or do not wish to carry out themselves. Hatch (1980) points out that this financial dependence is likely to cause strain between the grant giver and the voluntary agency. It also raises questions about the extent to which voluntary organizations can continue as 'voluntary,' self-governing bodies. Researchers have argued that the essence of voluntary action is its autonomy, but few have examined the influence of financial dependence on that autonomy:

> The essence of voluntary action is ... a question of independence and autonomy and its fundamental antithesis is statutory action, that is activity carried out under the aegis of local or central government and their associated agencies within the framework of statutory obligations laid down in legislation. By contrast, voluntary action is independent of state control and voluntary organizations are essentially those established and governed by their own members, without external interven-

tion. Independence, in the sense of self management, is the hallmark of voluntary action (Gladstone 1979:4).

Do Funding Policies Promote
Voluntary Sector Independence?

Against a background of financial restraint governments everywhere have been tightening the conditions for receipt of government funding. Contract funding is made available for specific tasks, or closely defined services, that government departments wish to purchase. In the last chapter it was pointed out that government is attempting to increase the accountability of these agencies by more rigorous methods of determining which individuals are eligible for contracted services. It is able to accomplish this through a system of closed referrals, in which only clients referred by the contracting department may be admitted to particular services.

Lipsky and Smith (1990) point out that voluntary organizations and government differ radically in their approach to providing services to clients. Government is driven by the need for equity, the principle that all clients within particular target groups receive a minimum standard of services that is equivalent in all geographical areas. Government applies equity standards so that the neediest will be served first when resources are scarce. When it needs to, government can also use equity standards to justify rationing services. Voluntary organizations, on the other hand, tend to be neighbourhood based. They provide services on a charitable basis and are more likely to focus on clients whose needs are compatible with their mission or central objectives. They are also more particular in their choice of clients in that some agencies are founded to serve specific constituencies or interest groups. It is therefore to be expected that they will be less committed to the government agenda that all clients within a specific target group receive services.

Lipsky and Smith (1990) also note that government departments and voluntary organizations respond differently to clients. Government contracts require that a client meet the focused criteria defined by government priorities before services are granted. Non-profit organizations are more likely to service clients on a first come first served basis, and any rationing mechanism is likely to be advisory rather than mandatory. Lipsky and Smith suggest that this tendency stems from the community-based nature of non-profit organizations. Workers usually know their clients personally and therefore resist reducing them to ciphers. In addition, non-profit organizations are often created in response to specific, local needs rather than to broad policy guidelines.

Another difference between the two sectors is the extent to which volunteers are involved. Government departments do not allow volunteers, whereas some voluntary agencies are totally reliant on them. Even those employing paid workers and professionals may recruit large numbers of volunteers, whose participation in voluntary organizations allows them to express their altruism. That professionals and other workers in the voluntary sector tend to be paid less than their counterparts in other sectors in BC suggests that these employees could also, in some respects, be considered to be volunteering part of their time. They may be attracted to the voluntary sector because the chance to exercise some power in decision-making offers a certain compensation for lower pay. Among other things, workers may be able to decide the types of clients who receive services. Voluntary sector employees may therefore view government attempts to establish client selection criteria as interference in the internal affairs of an agency.

Different approaches to client selection and services usually create potential conflict between government departments and voluntary agencies. The government views the non-profit method of client selection as inequitable. Voluntary agencies, on the other hand, see that the government's narrow eligibility criteria burden them with many more at-risk clients, who require intensive treatment. Many executive directors remarked that inappropriate clients were referred to their services. If they refused to accept these clients, however, the lack of referrals would be interpreted as a lack of demand for their services, and could lead to contract termination the following year, especially if the agency refused to modify services as requested. Often staff were not in a position to treat highly disturbed clients. An agency might set up one type of service only to find that different demands were made the following year. Executive directors maintained that their contracts were adjusted to emphasize those clients who were given a high priority under the government's rationing process. This represents not only a sharp shift in government funding methods but also a conflict with voluntary organizations' mission and founding vision as agencies of prevention, education, and early treatment:

> We can only provide services to those we are funded for. The ministry [MSS] is more strict now and their scope regarding who can receive services is much narrower.

We have a special needs contract. MSS is trying to refer too many difficult kids to our program. They are also trying to get us to take in kids from outside our region and we are refusing. We have a conflict because we want self referrals and MSS wants to do all the referrals.

We had to drop our group home. The provincial government would not fund our group home that had low attendance.

We are less responsive to our community. Before we had our own population that we provided services to. The parents would tell us what they wanted and we submitted a proposal to fund those needs. Now we no longer have any say in who comes to our services. We direct them to MSS.

The preventive approach gets no support from government. Our contracted services are geared to clients who need treatment.

An important way in which the government funding process influences agencies is by refusing funds for activities related to social change. The literature reviews the many pressures that fund providers place upon these organizations (Schechter 1982; Ng 1988; Ng, Walker, and Mueller 1990; Shragge 1990). The narrowing of eligibility criteria to 'needy' clients essentially reduces the ability of voluntary organizations to advocate for expanded resources to meet a wider set of needs. Wider eligibility criteria would create a situation in which many more individuals qualified for services but would be unable to receive them because of long waiting lists, thus legitimating the claim that not enough resources were being expanded. By narrowing the eligibility criteria and reducing the stream of clients through closed referrals, the government essentially reduces the political pressure for resource expansion.

Instead of funding the general purposes of an organization, external funders give monies for specific tasks or specific clients so that agencies focus on service delivery. This service orientation, with individuals as the primary focus, presents a shift from the broader focus of agencies, which had included prevention, education, community action, and early treatment. Shragge (1990) has therefore argued that although organizations had their origins in social movements aimed at social change, many are at risk of being co-opted as extensions of state programs and structures. Service delivery becomes a substitute for political action.

As voluntary organizations become more reliant on government funding they also become more vulnerable to changes in government funding priorities. Pfeffer and Salancik (1978) have theorized that in order to secure the resources necessary to survive, organizations will adapt their structure and change their goals. Government departments define the conditions under which organizations can be reimbursed for services. Most voluntary organizations maintain very broad mandates which enable them to subsume and respond quickly to the changing priorities and funding guidelines of government departments. They can shift the focus of their services as well as their target groups without appearing to change overall direction. It is also in their own interest to maintain broad mandates, considering that government policies lack explicit guidelines on long-term funding strategies and exhibit short term political reflexes. Some of those interviewed offered the following comments on the subject:

> We revised our mandate and made it more specific so that we could bid on contracts.

> We took on additional new services that were being funded by government.

> We used to provide services to all kinds of kids. Now we focus on children in conflict with the law.

> We could not continue with those services that always ended up in a deficit. We let those go and added new services that are being funded through privatization.

> Government cutbacks meant that we had to let go those services that were no longer funded. We expanded by going after contract funding.

> We switched our services and target groups to provide contracted services to families and children.

External funders also influence the management structure and operational procedures of voluntary organizations. The influence was indirectly alluded to in discussions with executive directors, who maintained that contract funding did not take administration costs into account. Managing grant funding is time consuming since grants are made available annually and are subject to review. The record-keeping and other accountability requirements of funders also affect the organization and management of agencies. In addition, government often calls the tune when it comes to participation in meetings and decision-making. Consultation between government and agencies usually follows a government agenda. To be effective, those in the voluntary sector must learn the culture of the public sector. Some executive directors commented as follows:

> Contracting has increased the amount of paperwork that we have to do. We also have to spend our time on public relations so that we know what other agencies are doing and what government is funding. Government is not prepared to pay for administration. It is difficult to get recognition for the long hours we work.

> We need a competent manager to deal with all the unpaid parts of the contract, like all this reporting and paperwork that we have to do.

> Our staff have to do all the administrative work related to contracts, in addition to providing services.

> We had to hire an administrator and a bookkeeper because of the increase in our workload.

Basoff (1982) identifies three stages in the evolution of community-based agencies. She argues that these stages are a response to pressures associated with funding from government and other sources. During the first phase, volunteers are extensively involved and there is a minimal amount of organizational formality. The second phase is characterized by increased organizational accountability and record-keeping but volunteers are still extensively involved in service delivery. In the third and final phase, the agency adopts traditional forms of fiscal and management practices and services are provided by trained professionals.

Some executive directors maintained that government refusal to fund administrative costs forced them to pay their staff low wages. The prevalence of low wages promotes the myth that poor pay in the sector is a sign of personal commitment. The alternative argument is that low wages force the voluntary sector to hire only low calibre personnel. Other executive directors, however, mentioned that their contracts included the standard administrative fee of 'between ten and fifteen per cent' that was recognized and paid for by government. These differences in experience may be related to economies of scale in contracting. If an agency managed a number of contracts the administration fee could be spread over all of them. If an agency managed only one or two contracts, the portion going to administration would be substantially higher.

Strategies to Maintain Voluntary Sector Autonomy
Contracting out gives voluntary organizations an integral role in service delivery. They also have more power than they would have in the marginal model, in which voluntary agencies are considered important, but peripheral to the government sector. While recognizing the dangers of their reliance on government funding, voluntary agencies are nevertheless attracted to such funds as a way to sustain or expand their agencies. Many executive directors commented that the more discretionary funding from United Way and the municipalities was not increasing. Contract funding was therefore crucial to the survival and growth of their agencies. Voluntary agencies are seeking to secure their own future by procuring contracts from as many government departments as they can. Diversifying their funding base ensures that total funding is not suddenly pulled from under their feet and enables voluntary agencies to exercise some choice over the range of services they will provide:

Contracting enabled us to survive. We can think of expanding because of contracting.

We wouldn't be here without contracts.

Contracting means that we get paid doing what we do. In the pre-contracting days we provided services but didn't always get paid. We were volunteers.

Our agency expanded because of contracting. Services have increased in the community. We have a better funding base to help cover overhead costs. Contracting develops a base from which further needs can be measured. Since the contracts are very specific in terms of the needs to be met, demand can be measured against contract definitions.

If you don't screw up, contracts usually get renewed. Stable funding lets us experiment. Our staff have a sense of security. We don't rely on one government department as in the pre-1980s. We were told in the 1980s to diversify our funding base.

Although contracting requirements and agency goals conflict on occasion, non-profit agencies can resort to various strategies. One possibility is to reject the norms imposed in contracts and risk losing the funding, although this jeopardizes the survival of the organization. One agency did refuse all contracts after providing contracted services for a number of years. Management felt that the agency had lost its community roots and had moved into crisis management for MSS. The executive director maintained that the involvement of the community, especially volunteers, was rejuvenated when contracts were refused, and that the agency became much more responsive to the community. This agency managed to survive without contracts because it received substantial funding from United Way, the City of Vancouver, and the federal government as well as its own fundraising.

Another strategy adopted by agencies was to accept contracts but attempt to change their conditions through bargaining and negotiation, to make them more amenable to agency goals. Contract funding was sought for services that were compatible with the mandate and other activities of the agency. Some agencies maintained that they retained great flexibility in designing programs and services. These agencies were more likely to be in the mentally handicapped field, or were providing very specialized services. Their expertise provided leverage in contract negotiations:

We own the houses and the ministry needs us. No one else can compete for these contracts as we own the property. Government is stuck with us.

We can manipulate terminology to meet the funding criteria.

We tailor our services knowing what is their funding priority. We have to present it in a way that is seen to fit their priority. We went after the Family Initiative money to pay for needed services – it supplements services which fit our mandate.

Yet another strategy is for the agency to make some of its objectives compatible with those of the funding department. This tactic involves seeking contracts while preserving the vision of the agency through mission-related activities and promotion of a community base. For example, one agency specializing in recreational services for youths sought contract funding for some treatment services. The amount of funding received for contracted services was peripheral and independent of that for recreational services.

Contracting has placed voluntary organizations in the difficult position of having to secure stable funding that does not restrict their autonomy. Because contract funding is by definition time limited, these organizations are without long-term guarantees of support. Attempting to secure stable funding while at the same time developing relationships with funders to demonstrate a balance of power, and with the community to demonstrate legitimacy, is a time-consuming task. Tension between the pressures of external funders and maintaining agency autonomy leads many agencies to yearn for some private endowment or wholly independent source of revenue.

Kramer (1986) cites several studies carried out in the United States showing little evidence that increased reliance on government funding in any way impeded agency autonomy. One reason may be the diversity of agency income. Diversity ensures that an agency is not totally dependent on any one source, which gives them some leverage when negotiating with government departments. Contracting with different government departments was already discussed as a possible method of diversification, but an agency in this position must still respond to government priorities. An important source of diversification, therefore, and one that gives agencies a greater degree of flexibility, is non-government funding. With fewer conditions attached to how money can be spent there is more scope for an agency to determine program and service priorities:

We can do whatever we like as long as we raise funds. We can't provide services to everybody unless we have core funding from government. Because we get only contract funding we have to do fundraising to provide services to those not covered under our contracts.

We have to raise funds as we can't get contract dollars to provide those services that we want to provide.

We have to do fundraising to support our non-contracted services. Our fundraising enables us to respond to our own needs and not just to government's perceived needs.

Fundraising prevents us from becoming too dependent on government.

The survival of our preventive programs depend on United Way funding, City funding and our own fundraising.

We've been doing fundraising to provide services beyond what our contracts stipulate. Our contracts do not provide funding for physiotherapy, speech therapy and transportation for all the children that come to our centre. We think these children need these services. Therefore we have to fundraise.

There are two main sources of nongovernment funding. The first is fundraising, which includes funds gained through membership fees, donations, rummage and bake sales, special event fundraising, and gaming activities such as casinos and bingos. (Given government controls and regulations over access and expenditure of gaming revenues, they would be more appropriately included under government funding, but all the agencies listed this funding source under their own fundraising and the analysis in this section follows this classification.) The second source of nongovernment revenue is fee-for-service, investment income, or other business charges such as renting out facilities, equipment, and resources.

Table 5.1 sets out the sources of nongovernment funding for ninety-seven non-profit agencies that receive provincial government funding through either grants only, contracts only, or both grants and contracts. Agencies receiving contracts were more dependent on government funding. Government funding from all three levels made up approximately 50 per cent of total funding for agencies receiving grants only, compared to 80 per cent for agencies receiving contracts or both grants and contracts. The table shows that agencies receiving only provincial government grant funding also received the largest share of their nongovernment funding from private and charitable giving (approximately 90 per cent). The other agencies raised more of their nongovernment funding from fee-for-service and other charges (roughly 60 per cent) than from private and charitable giving (about 40 per cent). The results in Table 5.1 also suggest that the proportion of funding from private and charitable giving increased marginally in the post-privatization period, which can be attributed to the greater significance of gaming revenue.

Table 5.1

Proportion of different sources of nongovernment funding by type of provincial funding in the pre- and post-privatization periods

	Govt. funding[1] Total funding	Nongovt. funding Total funding	Private and charitable giving[2] Nongovt. funding	Earned revenue and fee-for-service[3] Nongovt. funding
Agencies receiving prov. grants (10)				
Pre-privatization	51%	49%	93%	7%
Post-privatization	54	46	90	10
Agencies receiving prov. contracts (44)				
Pre-privatization	79	21	38	63
Post-privatization	78	22	42	58
Agencies receiving prov. grants and contracts (43)				
Pre-privatization	79	21	33	67
Post-privatization	78	22	38	61

[1] Includes funding from federal, provincial, and municipal governments.
[2] Includes United Way, donations, membership, fundraising from gaming, etc.
[3] Includes fee-for-service and other business charges.

The discussions with executive directors suggested that voluntary organizations respond in various ways to the influx of contract funding. Obviously, if an agency is not providing services under contract, and the agency receives small grants, fundraising is an important source of growth. It was not clear whether these agencies actively decided not to pursue contracts or whether they had not been successful in procuring them. Agencies that have had some success with contracting tend to then focus more energy on procuring more contracts. The discussions suggested that contracting provided greater benefits than did community fundraising in terms of agency growth and stability. For many agencies fundraising has become more and more closely associated with gaming activities, which again promise greater payoffs than community fundraising. For some agencies contract funding eliminated the pressure to fundraise. Their executive directors maintained that the availability of government funding meant that government was addressing many more needs. Service provision was more pressing and more rewarding than fundraising activity, which often did not lead to anything substantial. Other agencies saw fundraising as an important way to respond to community needs beyond what government was willing to pay. Yet others saw fundraising as an important way of involving the community with the agency, the amount raised indicating community support and legitimization. The variety of attitudes is indicated in the following responses:

Since we started receiving contract funding, we haven't felt the need to fundraise.

Our agency is relying less on fundraising and more on contracting.

No, we don't fundraise anymore. Government implied three years ago that our contract funding will be decreased if our fundraising is too successful.

We decreased our fundraising now that we have a stable funding base.

We're not so desperate now that we receive contract funding. We don't rely as much on fundraising.

Some societies have had their contract funding reduced because they receive so much gaming funding.

We have had to do less ... [fundraising]. We receive a lot of government money. Maybe this is interpreted by the board as the agency not needing to fundraise.

The message from government is that they won't pay 100 per cent of the cost of services. We have to fundraise. Most of our fundraising comes from bingos.

Funding from bingos is becoming our most stable source of revenue.

Our contracts are considered in light of our gaming revenues. Our gaming revenues subsidize our administration costs.

The results reviewed above indicate that executive directors perceive fundraising revenue as having an influence on their contract negotiations. Although contract rates are determined through the bargaining process, other factors come into play. Newer organizations, perceiving that contracts are awarded to the lowest bidder, and wanting to secure ongoing funding, are more likely to bid low to begin with. Once they have secured a contract, these organizations may either continue to struggle with ongoing problems associated with inadequate funding, or they may be able to negotiate higher rates depending upon their expertise in negotiations as well as monopoly in service provision. Some executive directors implied that they were not reimbursed the full costs because government officials expected them to make up the difference through fundraising. This perception that they were subsidizing government may have discouraged some societies from fundraising. Many refused to engage in fundraising at all, while others refused to participate in community fundraising, preferring to concentrate on gaming revenues such as from bingos and casinos. Since the number of times a society can access such revenue is controlled by government, this limits how much is raised through gaming. These reasons perhaps explain the smaller proportion of nongovernment funding raised from private and charitable giving by those organizations that rely more heavily on government contracted funding.

Community fundraising is also very time consuming, requiring much volunteer and staff effort without any guarantee of substantial results. Many agencies saw fundraising activities as detracting from their important service-providing responsibilities. In addition, managing a multi-service agency dependent on contracts from different levels of government, as well as government departments, makes the administration of these agencies much more complex. Executive directors and paid staff do not have the time to recruit volunteers and engage in public relations in the community. In addition, members of boards of directors of these societies may be against fundraising because they view it as a way of letting government off the hook. Board members are also reluctant to become involved in community fundraising, again because of time commitments. Many of the agencies do not have the funds to hire a professional fundraiser. Thus, gaming becomes attractive because it requires predictable amounts of time from volunteers and staff, and the income it generates tends to be much more substantial than the proceeds from community fundraising. Some agencies, however, struggle with the moral dilemma of participating in such activities. Some executive directors made these comments:

Fundraising should not be part of a direct service agency's activities. We should be free to provide services.

These are basic core services that should be funded through core funding from government. Government expects us to play bingo and blackjack so that we can get these poor people to pay for the services they get from us the next morning.

We don't think non-profits should be fundraising. We're making it easy for government to not provide adequate funding for essential services. How can we think of taking part in bingos and casinos? Those people that come through our doors for services are the very ones you find in the bingo halls.

It is really difficult to get our board to do fundraising.

We have brought in a professional fundraiser because United Way and City funding are not growing and represents a decreasing proportion of our revenue base.

As was seen in Table 5.1, agencies that receive either contract or both contract and grant funding from the provincial government derive approximately 60 per cent of their nongovernment funding from fee-for-service activities and other business charges.[1] Voluntary agencies that do not engage in fundraising – or whose fundraising dollars are tied to contract funding or pay for administrative costs – must themselves finance those services for which the government is not prepared to pay, through fee-for-service or applying a self-financing criterion. In other words, a service is not provided unless it pays for itself. Cutbacks and greater restrictions on government funding have moved voluntary organizations in this direction. In 1984, for example, government withdrew its funding to an agency that was operating a drop-in centre for mothers and tots. The agency responded by converting the drop-in into a child-minding service for which there was an hourly charge. This hourly charge, together with a small grant from the city, enabled the agency to sustain the service on a self-financing basis.

Similarly, another agency had its core funding for a seniors centre withdrawn in 1984. This section of the agency survived through contract funding from the Ministry of Health and a subsidy from the agency's fundraising revenues. It became more self-sufficient through a program in which one staff member and a group of twenty-five volunteers helped seniors with their yearly tax forms. This service was provided for a nominal fee to those who frequented the centre.

Another agency had received core funding from government in the early 1970s to run a legal aid clinic. In 1984, core funding was cut back and the agency had to reduce its staff. The agency maintained that prior to 1984 it had more flexibility to determine who was eligible for legal aid services. After 1984, criteria became less flexible, and although the agency continued to provide services to those not eligible for legal aid, it levied a nominal user fee determined on a sliding scale. Some costs had to be recovered even from clients eligible for legal aid. Legal services on a fee-for-service basis were also extended to clients using other services of the agency.

Some agencies that refused to fundraise took on private paying clients. One agency providing homemaking services, for example, extended these services to private clients. It also established a housecleaning service. Another agency that provided services for clients with special needs established a rental service for aids and technical equipment relating to such needs. Some agencies experimented with fee-for-service based on demands made by clients. For example, one agency found that clients were requesting counselling services for which it could not secure funding. It established a counselling service for which a charge was levied. Many low-income clients could not afford the charges and the person hired then had to work part time on a contracted service as well. Many educational programs, such as parenting classes and workshops, result from requests from clients of the agency. The agency may levy a nominal charge for these services.

Some agencies incurred a deficit because they did not believe that clients should be charged for services. The agencies able to take this approach were usually somewhat successful at community fundraising, or practised economies of scale that enabled them to subsidize these services. Nevertheless, they usually sustained the services in this manner for limited periods of time only, during which they attempted to secure funding. If the agency was not successful in securing some funding the service was relinquished or a fee was levied.

Thus, it could be argued that the government's privatization strategy has been successful in that it has encouraged a further extension of market principles as a basis for rationing or distributing social services. While the voluntary sector has so far avoided the development of a two-tiered social service system by levying minimal charges, movement toward such a system could escalate if government freezes or decreases its funding levels. Individuals and families will bear more financial responsibility, especially since those who cannot afford to pay, or who do not fit the increasingly residual public sector criteria, will have to rely on the informal sector.

Weisbrod (1989) and others (U.S. Small Business Administration 1984) have argued that reductions in government funding are forcing an increasing number of voluntary organizations to seek new sources of funding by engaging in activities that one associates with the free market. The results presented in this text indicate that voluntary agencies that deliver contracted services are also having to charge a fee-for-service or to establish a self-financing basis to serve their own constituents.

In the context of their nongovernment funding, voluntary organizations in BC are possibly becoming increasingly differentiated according to whether they fit the fee-dominant or the charity-dominant model. In the fee-dominant model, income is derived from fees and other charges. In the charity-dominant model, their largest source of revenue is private giving from individuals, foundations, corporations and, increasingly in British Columbia, gaming revenues. Hansmann (1989) argues that by the turn of the century, non-profit organizations will increasingly be categorized in this way.

The reasons for their pursuit of such revenues are complex and form the basis of an ongoing debate. Lifset (1989) and James (1983) discuss the cross-subsidization model as one explanation for the tendency of voluntary organizations to provide services on a fee-for-service basis. Cross-subsidization refers to the practice of using revenues from another source to subsidize deficit-producing activities. Lifset differentiates among three types of business-related activities undertaken by this sector: (1) fee-for-service; (2) unrelated business activities; (3) related business activities. Services for which fees are levied are usually mission related. However, the recipients of that service are also the source of financial support. Unrelated business activities refer to those services that are not related to the basic mission of the organization. For example, if the organization has facilities that are not used at certain times, those facilities may be rented out to generate revenues. The organization may also undertake ventures that utilize its existing physical capital and organizational expertise. Related commercial or business activities are those that serve the auxiliary purposes of the organization. These are typically provided to serve the different constituencies of a non-profit organization. Examples include gift shops attached to museums, health clubs attached to the YMCA, and so on. Activities of the third type – related business activities – have led small businesses to accuse non-profit organizations of unfair competition.

Another reason given for the pursuit of commercial activities by non-profit agencies is that the demand for services once funded by philanthropy exceeds available sources of such funding (Hansmann 1989). The results presented in this text support the notion that charitable giving through the United Way, while increasing, now makes up a much smaller proportion of the funding available to these organizations than in the early 1980s. Revenues from the agencies' own fundraising activities have increased substantially. However, they cannot match the growth of government funding received by the sector. Crimmins and Keil (1983) suggest that the pressure on voluntary organizations to develop management and accounting practices to deal with the complexities of their growth has helped to blur the distinction between government and the sector, and also between business and the non-profit sector.

As non-profit agencies increasingly engage in business-related activities, their tax-exempt status comes under greater scrutiny. The Interpretation Bulletin (IT-496) issued by Revenue Canada defines the conditions under which a non-profit organization is exempt from corporate income tax.[2] The organization may not retain excess profits and may not pay them out to any member of the organization. The surplus must be used in ways associated with the organization. Salaries, wages, fees, or honoraria for services to the organization are not included. In light of these conditions Krashinsky (1986) argues that there would be no problem for an entrepreneur to set up as a non-profit organization and arrange to be paid as an executive director. Hurl and Tucker (1986) have also pointed out that such developments are likely if suppliers perceive that governments prefer dealing with non-profits. Hansmann (1989) questions the continuation of tax-exempt status for non-profit organizations when some of the services provided by these organizations are no different from those offered by for-profit firms. He argues that many non-profit organizations are in essence for-profit firms in disguise. Non-profit status offers these organizations greater control, protection from competition, and greater financial returns. On the other hand, 'remedies' on inequalities claimed by small business could have far-reaching implications for both the public and non-profit sector. Policy limiting such activities could reduce the scope of non-profit services and 'we will have both fewer sacred cows and fewer cash cows' (Lifset 1989:164).

These developments have an important bearing on the way in which non-profit organizations are evolving in British Columbia. Non-profit organizations engaging in fee-for-service activities make it easier for the government to expect that people will pay for services if it should withdraw financial support to the voluntary sector. More restricted targeting of government funds in an effort to stabilize or reduce government expenditures comes at a time when demographic and social developments – an aging population, more single-parent families – indicate growing demand for the expansion of social welfare services. Thus, it is clear that market principles will increasingly be used to ration and distribute services through the 1990s and beyond.

Summary
Contracting out gives the non-profit sector a much more important role in service delivery, but it also raises questions about the extent to which government influences the activities and direction of the sector. Voluntary organizations are walking a tightrope, trying to balance their need for public support with their own identity and independence.

The chapter examined the influence exerted by funders and the strategies available to the voluntary sector to counteract these influences. Retaining and competing for contracts from different levels of government as well as different government departments are strategies used by these organizations to diversify their funding base. However, managing these contacts has also transformed these organizations into more complex structures. Increasing management responsibilities, together with the difficulties associated with community fundraising, are pushing these societies to rely on gaming revenues as a source of nongovernment funding. Since government controls the number of times an organization can access such revenues, this necessarily limits what these societies can raise through gaming. At the same time, government cutbacks and greater restrictions on government funding have moved voluntary organizations in a fee-for-service or self-financing direction to serve constituents who fall outside government criteria. The rhetoric of partnership seems to be concerned not only with an alternative delivery system for social services, but also with the transformation of established patterns of responsibility in social service finance.

6
Conclusion

Voluntary organizations are an important part of our society. Studying them, however, is not a simple task, because the voluntary sector corresponds to the multifarious needs of society: it contains many different types of organizations involved in a blend of activities that defy clear definition. Voluntary organizations invoke images of community, neighbour-helping-neighbour, and civic dependability – images which have exerted a powerful influence on popular support of this sector. The contemporary reality, however, is that these organizations are playing an increasing role in delivering social services on government's behalf under purchase-of-service agreements.

Attempts by neoconservative governments to stabilize or reduce government expenditure in the 1980s fostered a policy of privatization. This was intended to return a larger share of the responsibility for social welfare services to private hands. Greater reliance on the voluntary sector, as advocated by neoconservatives, must therefore be interpreted within the context of its potential for reducing the role of the state. Those with sympathies in the direction of state collectivism have also been influenced by a negative assessment of the achievements of the centralized, professionalized, and bureaucratized services of the welfare state. They view voluntary agencies as important mediating structures that can bring about decentralized and more responsive services to people. Both political sides claim that in this manner local democracy can be extended and citizens empowered because they would have a greater say in services. Neoconservatives and state collectivists, representing distinct and opposing ideological positions on the role of government in society, are therefore virtually indistinguishable in their support of a greater role for the voluntary sector.

This pattern of public support is raising new questions about the relative roles of the voluntary, government, and private sectors. The parallel bars and extension ladder models proposed by the Webbs (1912) are useful in describing the evolving role of voluntary organizations in British Columbia. Voluntary organizations in the province followed the parallel bars model until the 1960s. With some exceptions (such as the Children's Aid Society), voluntary organizations played a marginal role and provided services parallel to those of government but for a different clientele. The dramatic expansion of federal and provincial government responsibility in social welfare in the 1950s and 1960s was seen by most observers as occurring at the expense of other social institutions, especially non-profit organizations. Focus on the expansion of the public sector, however, has left the elaborate network of collaboration between the two sectors in the shadow. This collaboration laid the foundations for voluntary organizations to become partners with government in the policy shift toward privatization.

Beginning in the early 1970s, the NDP government of British Columbia encouraged a more central role for voluntary organizations. The government provided funding to promote integration between government services and innovative community initiatives that met emerging needs. During this period, voluntary organizations provided services that fitted the Webbs' extension ladder model (1912), in which government provides the basic framework of services and the voluntary sector carries these services to 'finer shades' of social advancement.

The rhetoric of privatization by the BC Social Credit government in the 1980s seemed to indicate that there would be a revival of the parallel bars model. In this model, government minimizes its responsibilities and leaves the provision of social welfare to volunteers, self-help groups, private charity, and the commercial sector. Evidence from the survey presented in this text indicates that the Social Credit government embraced the idea of competition and market economics as the means to achieve cost effectiveness, more choice, and better service. It is clear that the private sector (self-employed individuals and entrepreneurial organizations) has been given a somewhat enlarged role in service provision, but the government has also increased its reliance on the voluntary sector. In doing so, it has accepted the concepts of decentralization and empowerment inherent in the welfare pluralism model. There is thus a certain ambiguity about the essential thrust of government policy committed to contracting out.

The provincial Ministry of Social Services funding of the voluntary sector was assessed to determine whether government spending for contracted-out services has decreased, given that expenditure reduction was one of the declared objectives. Under these circumstances, delegation of service delivery to the voluntary sector would constitute a dismantling of the social services. In fact, government expenditure showed an increase in the seven-year period under study, but the rate of growth was much slower in the post-privatization period than in the period before. The policy of restraint gave government the opportunity to limit its direct service role to the statutory responsibilities of child protection and income maintenance, and to contract out any direct service provision, including new programs developed for the mentally ill and the juvenile populations.

Official policies in operation have not yet matched what government intended in its policy rhetoric. It is entirely possible that the Social Credit government, believing that it would have another term in office, proceeded cautiously while trying to build up popular support for its radical agenda of reducing expenditures on the social services. A gradual slowing down of expenditures is perhaps preferable because it sustains the illusion that government supports collective social services, even though the level of funding may be inadequate to maintain standards or to meet new and emerging demands. Therborn (1984) has argued that governments' inability to appreciably reduce social expenditures presents evidence that the welfare state is irreversible. However, Mishra (1989) points out that a frontal assault on expenditure is not the only option open to governments committed to a neoconservative agenda of reducing services to a minimum. Selective cutbacks, limiting expenditure growth, and privatization are other methods that can be used to erode services. In British Columbia the policy shift to privatization has meant that private non-profit and for-profit organizations provide publicly mandated and funded services under purchase-of-service agreements. Although expenditure has continued to increase for these programs, albeit more slowly, the potential for neoconservative policy to further erode these programs remains considerable.

When the rate of government spending growth slows, or when eligibility for government-funded services is made more rigid, demand does not simply disappear. Instead there is a shift from public services to private: to the commercial sector, if there is ability to pay; or to the informal sector, where care is provided even without payment, generally by female relatives. Service provision through voluntary organizations may make it easier for governments to exploit the informal sector, since these agencies have a long history of working with volunteers and communities interested in altruistic effort. Savings can be realized through the gradual substitution of lower paid staff, volunteers, unpaid staff, and informal care by women. Thus government expenditure in social services will become more 'efficient' and 'economic' simply because it is inadequate (Opit 1977).

The BC government continues to fund social services but the delivery of these services has been delegated to third parties. Developments in the 1980s saw the emergence of an overall philosophy about the public sector in which government explicitly saw itself in an enabling role, concerned with contracting out and regulation of agencies under contract. While voluntary organizations appear to play an important role in social service delivery in British Columbia, it is difficult to monitor the flow of public funds to this sector compared to others for there does not exist a central registry of government contracts. The 1993 Korbin Report on the public service is critical of the rapid growth of commercial and consultant contracting, suggesting that this decision was based on an ideological preference of past administrations rather than an analysis of value for money. As a result, thousands within this shadow civil service have been reclassified as employees, and it is recommended that 'the government establish standards for comparison of proposed contracting costs to costs of providing services using direct government resources' (Korbin Report 1993:55). This report may bring about important changes in the overall philosophy of the public sector developed under the Social Credit government.

In the second volume the Korbin inquiry includes 'Community Contracted Social Services' under the public sector defined as organizations and institutions that are funded primarily by government to provide services to the public but operate at arm's length from government. The report therefore raises the question of whether such contracted services provided by non-profit organizations should be seen as public sector services. (A further question is whether those voluntary organizations that participated in the consultation process to this inquiry also view themselves as part of the public sector.) Legislation following this inquiry would establish an employers' association in each public sector: health, contracted community social services, education, colleges and institutes, universities, crown corporations, and the civil service. Each sector would nominate a representative to the Public Sector Employers Council which would also be composed of up to seven provincial cabinet ministers, including the finance minister.

The broad thrust of the commission is to develop consistent compensation and employment practices throughout the civil service and the public sector, and to enable government to take control over government spending. These developments indicate that the voluntary sector may become more directly accountable to government. The broadening of the MSS mandate anticipated in new legislation, as well as other initiatives to foster community involvement in service planning and service delivery, may call into question the appropriateness of the purchase-of-service contract model. It may become increasingly difficult to distinguish between government and the organized voluntary sector.

The voluntary sector has, as this study shows, always played an important role in social service delivery in British Columbia. However, there is no coherent theory that specifies the role of the voluntary sector vis-à-vis government provision. Writers have also tended to fuse the two sectors when describing the social welfare system in British Columbia. The changed reality, referred to in Chapter 2, was the catalyst that saw the voluntary sector assume a much more important role in service delivery. Those supporting welfare pluralism and an increased voluntary sector role base their arguments on community action, empowerment, and participation. Beresford and Croft (1984) suggest that these same arguments are advanced by the New Right, which favours reprivatization and returning responsibility to self-help groups, individuals, and communities.

In developing their model, welfare pluralists focus on the failings of the welfare state and ignore the structural elements that determine poverty and inequality in society. They fail to acknowledge that increased government intervention resulted from the failings of the market and voluntary action in the first place. Whether the emergence of arguments for community action, empowerment, and decentralization has resulted in a major expansion in the number of voluntary organizations is as yet unclear, but there has been a greater commitment to consumerism in social services. Citizen involvement and client rights are increasingly couched in the market vocabulary of consumer rights, consumer choice, and consumer sovereignty.

One argument underpinning support for the private sector has been that increasing this version of 'public choice' will lead to self-regulation. Consumers will be able to effect change through their purchasing ability and their power to switch allegiance. It is evidently clear, however, that the relative share of the different suppliers in the social service market has taken little account of people's preferences, and is instead largely determined by government policy. It is also questionable whether consumers have any real choice if government spending cuts mean that there is not enough funding to meet needs, or if spending is targeted to specific client groups.

Diminishing social expenditures also bring into question the ability of government to regulate other service providers. Can it maintain control as its own provision dwindles and it becomes dependent on the other suppliers of service? The possibility of unequal safeguards for clients depending on which sector supplies the service must be raised. This is an important issue in light of Bill C-69, which limits the growth of federal transfer payments for social services, health, and education, and which is likely to encourage the growth of more private provision.

These developments also raise questions about the role of the voluntary sector in the welfare state. The evidence shows that provincial government funding is the most important source of funding for non-government organizations. While the proportion of provincial government funding received by non-profit agencies in 1982-3 and 1988-9 was about the same (75 per cent approximately), contract funding for statutory and related services became more important in the latter period. In contract funding, the government sets the terms of reference and funds agencies to provide that service. Government departments thus move their own clients to top priority for social services. Clients who might have been served by non-profit groups are therefore less likely to receive publicly subsidized services. Purchase-of-service contracts enlist voluntary organizations as 'partners' with government. However, this increased role in service delivery may be at the expense of those characteristics for which this sector is valued. These organizations have traditionally played a role in confronting the state by pointing out deficiencies and inequalities in government provision, in expanding the range of potential responses to any given social problems by offering alternatives to government provision, and in integrating individuals to communities by acting as mediating structures.

Another important issue is how the degree of dependence on government sources of finance affects the relationship between government and the voluntary sector. Government depends on non-profit agencies to deliver services on its behalf, while non-profit agencies depend on government funding to secure their own future. This mutual dependence is now fashionably referred to as a 'partnership.' Both sides prefer to minimize their dependence and to see themselves instead as independent buyers and sellers of human services in an 'arm's length' relationship. Since government controls the funding on which the voluntary sector increasingly depends, however, there is hardly a balance of power. Although government claims to view the relationship as a partnership, the notion must ring a little hollow to voluntary organizations, which live under the shadow of having their admission and service eligibility criteria changed annually in contract negotiations.

The heterogeneity of voluntary organizations suggests that their relationship with government varies with their organizational development. Some societies, for example, are like government service departments in that they are totally funded by government and services are delivered by professionals. These organizations are wholly concerned with contracting and with little connection to the wider values claimed by the sector. At the other extreme are almost wholly volunteer-based organizations with only a small proportion of government funding. In between are those that receive government and nongovernment funding to deliver services for government as well as services related to their mission. As they receive more government contract funding it is critical whether these organizations operate according to government-determined needs or the community of interest from which they arise.

Voluntary organizations that raise some of their own resources while at the same time contracting to deliver services on government's behalf obviously have more leverage in the partnership than those that are totally dependent on government funding. In this the larger, more experienced societies have the advantage. But is the diversity of the voluntary sector recognized in government policies? The reality is that although some organizations in the voluntary sector work more closely with government, for the most part the two sectors operate as if they were entirely separate. Yet the notion of partnership conjures up images of joint responsibility for planning, policy-making, and implementation.

Government seems to have adopted an ad hoc approach to support for the sector. Funding seems to be a product of history and is more and more frequently determined by limits set by the Treasury. Voluntary organizations need funding strategies that provide stable revenues so that they can develop effective and dependable services. Certainty, flexibility, and continuity of funding contribute to greater effectiveness. At issue is how government and the voluntary sector are to resolve the apparent contradiction between voluntary organizations' need for stable funding and the government's wish to promote efficiency through competition in the tendering process. Given the organizational diversity of the voluntary sector, what strategy should the government adopt in funding its development? In the government's quest for efficiency and cost effectiveness it may opt to contract only with voluntary agencies that demonstrate economies of scale. Resolution of funding issues will significantly affect the ways in which government can enable voluntary organizations to provide integrated, coordinated services of the same level, quality, and coverage across geographical boundaries. Kramer (1985) maintains that, while there are recurring demands for community empowerment and the removal of bureaucratized systems, lack of access, coherence, continuity, and coordination can be found in most advanced welfare states, regardless of their mixture of public and private service providers. While the growth of public provision has not solved these major problems of fragmentation and lack of coordination, a more private system exacerbates these problems through duplication and competition. Culpitt (1982) therefore argues that decisions on social policy will continue to be made, as they have in the past, on the basis of political considerations.

The scale of government funding to the voluntary sector suggests that the future of the sector is inextricably tied to the future of the welfare state. It is obvious that the sector cannot return to philanthropy, the traditional source of funding for such agencies. Voluntary organizations are now, in fact, part of the welfare state. Nevertheless, the sector needs consolidation if it is to participate in this partnership in any meaningful way. Voluntary agencies need to organize themselves in a way that will allow public bodies to understand the diversity of the sector. Only in so doing will the sector be able to communicate with its different constituencies. Voluntary organizations must learn to act together in order to include their sector in dialogue with authorities in such matters as value for money, accountability, fair practice, monitoring, and evaluation. Organization of this sort has already occurred in the mental handicap field, and attests to the significance of intermediary bodies in helping affiliated organizations with political skills and constituents with policies to protect themselves.

Currently, voluntary organizations outside the mental handicap field may be consulted on planning and policy issues in an ad hoc way. Key individuals may play an important role and often it is not clear what sector or constituency they represent. Pluralists have argued that voluntary organizations are important mediating structures that can empower the disenfranchised. It is difficult to understand how consumers engaged in decision-making in these mediating structures can feel more enfranchised in a political sense, as intimated by pluralists, when the sector need not be included in the decision-making process at all, except in an advisory capacity. Government employees call the tune when it comes to participation in and consultation about the government agenda. To be effective, outsiders have to learn the language, procedures, and culture of the public sector. This situation engenders elitism since only those who have the training or long-term experience can be included. Consultations and service planning, when they do occur, involve government officials and the elites of the voluntary sector.

Despite these concerns, voluntary organizations have flocked to government contract funding. Without it many agencies would have difficulty surviving and doing their work. Even so, many executive directors of voluntary organizations claim that changing government priorities force them to change their service aims and objectives. Non-compliance with government requests usually leads to loss of that contract and a scramble for other funding to save programs and ensure the survival of the agency.

Contracting out may solve the current contradiction in which the general populace wants more government services but less government. It is possible that government's preoccupation with an alternative political model of less government allows it to solve the dilemma described by Berger and Neuhaus 'to address human needs without exacerbating the reasons for animus against the welfare state' (1979:2). The mix of private and public activities in contracting out may enable government to extend its influence and control in the private sector while masking government growth and making it more acceptable to the populace. Government may not directly manage voluntary organizations, but it exerts considerable influence on their activities through purchase-of-service agreements with tightly controlled conditions attached to funding. The distinction between the two sectors thus becomes less sharp.

Increased government funding has been accompanied by more government control over who is eligible for government-funded services. From the perspective of the voluntary sector, tighter funding control is accompanied by contract negotiations that focus on the bottom line of the budget. Funding is crucial to the calibre of staff hired, the staff-client ratio, and the condition of the physical plant, all vital components of quality. However, variations in contract remuneration rates received by these agencies between and within regions, as well as between and within program areas, raise questions about the quality and standards of service that are fostered by the purchase-of-service contracting model.

The evidence reveals that all external funders require some financial and service reporting. Process accountability is left largely to the discretion of the government staff managing a particular contract, and varies according to the staffing level of the department and the relationship with the agency delivering the services. Program accountability is intermittent. Although conditions specifying eligibility requirements are more specific, monitoring and evaluation procedures lack a consistent and coherent framework. It could be that government, in valuing the diversity and innovation of this sector, wants to appear to give agencies considerable freedom of action.

The voluntary sector also expressed differing views about what constituted appropriate accountability requirements from external funders. There was great variation in experience from contract to contract, from department to department, and from issue to issue. Some agencies wanted more standardized, written guidelines while others viewed these as undue interference. It is of concern that in the absence of mutually agreeable terms of accountability both sides focus their energies on the balance of power instead of on developing and delivering effective services. The two sides need to agree on fair practice, effectiveness, value for money, and so on in order to foster a good working relationship. In establishing the terms of reference for their partnership, both sides need to recognize that public funders have to answer to their own constituents and that the voluntary sector must demonstrate its responsibility to both the funder and the community.

Their closer relationship with the government is likely to encourage voluntary organizations to develop into formal, rational bureaucratic structures. Whether the sector will then lose those features for which it is valued – innovation and flexibility – is an important question. It is also possible that some organizations within the organized voluntary sector will assume quasi-governmental status, enabling them to deliver government services in a coherent, coordinated, and comprehensive manner. The smaller, less organized, and more volunteer-based voluntary organizations may carry on the type of work for which the sector is valued. But who should finance the voluntary sector when its work is valued by the community at large but does not fit closely with government mandates?

The drive for economic efficiency in the social services is not accompanied by the same concern for effectiveness. In fact, the needs and satisfaction of clients are given scant attention in contract negotiations or in the monitoring and evaluation of services. Privatization appears to be motivated by the desire to reduce government, and does not address the issue of how service delivery through voluntary organizations can promote greater equity and social justice. Economic efficiency is associated with social equity even though it is clear that little effort has been made to determine priorities based on need.

It can be argued that one of the intended consequences of privatization is the importation of market principles into the social services. By tightening its eligibility criteria and its referral system, government has ensured that those who can afford to pay will purchase these services in the private market. Those who cannot afford to do so will rely on the informal sector or on increasingly residual publicly funded social services. Increasing management responsibilities, together with the difficulties associated with community fundraising, are pushing these non-profit societies to rely on gaming revenues as an important source of nongovernment funding. Because government controls access to gaming revenues, and influences how such revenues can be spent, non-profit agencies are finding that they must provide services on a fee-for-service or a self-financing basis if they wish to serve their own constituents outside government-defined criteria. Within this context, Judge (1982) and Walker (1984a) argue that privatization represents an attempt not only to establish a new balance between public and private provision but also to restructure the balance between public and private financing of social services.

As the distinction between the government and non-profit sectors becomes obscured, so does the distinction between the business and non-profit sectors. Declining charitable and philanthropic funds, combined with stricter eligibility for government-funded services, are compelling non-profit organizations to provide services on a self-financing basis to their own constituents. Their involvement in service provision rationed through the market criteria is raising questions, as it has in the United States, over whether non-profit agencies are becoming like their commercial counterparts and whether they should still be entitled to public policy and tax advantages. The pursuit of commercial activities may allow non-profit organizations to retain their independence and to respond to their constituencies but it may also, in the end, lead these agencies to lose sight of their mission and ultimately their legitimacy.

Thus, it can be argued that the BC government is encouraging the development of the private sector on grounds of efficiency without considering the implications for social equity and social justice. In addition, delegating service delivery to voluntary organizations may make it easier for the government to dismantle the social services through a process of resource starvation. The study presented in this text suggests that although the contracting process espouses economic efficiency, it does not follow the competitive market model. Contracting out may simply allow the government to reduce the size of the public sector.

These developments indicate that future options for the voluntary sector are critically determined by future trends in welfare expenditure. Despite the rhetoric, successive provincial governments in British Columbia have been constrained by legislation that defines their mandate, by overarching rules of the provincial budget set by the Treasury, and by funding arrangements with the federal government. The federal government's commitment to deficit reduction has witnessed a shift away from universalism toward greater targeting of social programs, as demonstrated by developments relating to Family Allowance and Old Age Security. The possibility of user fees in medicare indicates a step in a similar direction. The future of social programs is also being shaped by federal transfer payments to the provinces suggesting that regional disparities may be an issue. The capping of transfer payments under the Canada Assistance Plan and Established Program Funding, and anticipated changes to equalization payments represent a widespread restructuring of the welfare system that is expected to bring about a substantial review of entitlement to services. In addition, the globalization of our economic policies through the free trade agreement with the U.S., and with the U.S. and Mexico under the North American Free Trade Agreement (NAFTA) indicate that Canadian social programs will face increasing pressure to harmonize with those in the U.S. and Mexico. The NAFTA agreement stipulates that public services should be treated like commodities subject to market competition. Further, commercialized management of health care and social services will be allowed, with important ramifications for the non-profit sector. Preoccupation with the deficit, along with new demographic and social trends that promise to expand the need for social services, suggest that market criteria to ration and distribute social services will continue to expand.

Appendices

Appendix 1: Methodology

The purpose of this research is to examine the changing roles of the government and the non-profit sector in funding and delivering social services to families and children in British Columbia. The research examines the implications for the voluntary sector as it assumes what appears to be a major role in delivering these services.

From the Pilot Study to the Expanded Study

The pilot study examined the impact of restraint on fifty-eight non-profit agencies in three communities. The expanded study continued to track patterns of funding from different sources to the non-profit sector. It focused on the implications for the voluntary sector as it extends its role, through purchase-of-service agreements, to deliver services on government's behalf.

The Sampling Frame

To represent the province, the survey covered the following geographical areas:

(1) The Capital Regional District (CRD) and the Greater Vancouver Regional District (GVRD) represented the two major metropolitan areas. Sumas, Matsqui, and Abbotsford, suburban areas abutting the GVRD, were also included with the large metropolitan communities.

(2) Four medium-sized urban communities were included: Prince George (Northern Interior), Kelowna (Okanagan), Kamloops (South Central), and Nanaimo (Central Vancouver Island).

(3) Six smaller towns represented the small communities. These were selected on the basis that they represented different parts of the province: Quesnel (Cariboo), Nelson (Kootenay Central),

Cranbrook (Kootenay West), Terrace (Northwest), Dawson Creek (Peace River, North East), and the Fraser Valley (a suburban semi-rural area approximately an hour and a half's drive from Vancouver). The Fraser Valley (incorporating Sumas, Matsqui, and Abbotsford) was subsequently included as part of the GVRD because the agency data revealed trends more comparable to the GVRD than to small towns.

The BC provincial ministries of Social Services and Housing, Health, and Attorney General provided lists of all agencies, individuals, and companies that the government funds for social service delivery. From this comprehensive listing a statistically valid sample was drawn for each of the geographical areas in the study. Specifically, the Community and Family Health Services Division of the Ministry of Health, and the Corrections Division and Community Program Division of the Ministry of the Attorney General, provided lists of individuals and/or agencies receiving contract funding. The Ministry of Social Services and Housing provided a listing of contracts drawn from the entire child care portfolio. Contracts were identifiable by program areas, region, and dollar amount.

Sampling

The lists received from the three ministries were reduced into a mutually exclusive listing of agencies for each of the areas included in this study. If an agency provided services in several program areas, its name would appear several times on this list. The original lists did not show any consistency; sometimes the agency contracting to provide the service would be listed, and sometimes the project name would be listed. Matching agency to project would have been facilitated if addresses were consistently available. Matchings proved most difficult for residential care services, commonly referred to as children-in-care resources.

Children-in-care resources were usually listed by the name of the resource (the name of a group home, for example) rather than the organization with which it was affiliated. The names of resources, or the programs under which they were listed, provided no clue as to whether they might be operated by private individuals, companies, or non-profit agencies. In addition, telephone numbers were not listed, in order to protect the clients in these resources.

Sorting the children-in-care resources into those operated privately and those operated by an identified non-profit agency was easier outside the two major metropolitan areas, perhaps because agencies in smaller communities tend to play a generalist role and therefore have more contact with other major players in social services. These agencies had access to information that their counterparts in larger communities might not share.

Ministry of Social Services staff members were approached for help in identifying which of the large number of children-in-care resources in the GVRD and CRD were non-profit. For each resource, MSS staff also provided the name of the agency, contact persons, and telephone numbers. This made it possible not only to establish a verified mutually exclusive listing of non-profit agencies, but also to consider interviewing a convenient sample of the privately operated resources.

The listings provided by the ministries of Health and Attorney General were matched against the verified Ministry of Social Services listing to produce the final set of mutually exclusive agencies. It was clear that the majority of agencies contracted with MSS.

Agencies that contracted with the ministries of Health or Attorney General (AG) were also likely to contract with the Social Services ministry. All those agencies contracting with Health and AG but not with Social Services (less than 10 per cent) were included in the sample. In regions outside the two major metropolitan areas their inclusion was automatic with a 100 per cent sampling. In the GVRD, CRD, and Fraser Valley, agencies contracting only with the Health and AG ministries were automatically included in the sample selected. The remainder was randomly selected using a table of random numbers.

Appendix Table A.1 shows the number of non-profit agencies identified in each area included in the study. Because of the small number of agencies providing services in the small and medium-sized communities, there was a 100 per cent sampling in these areas. Because so many agencies were identified in the Greater Vancouver Regional District, they were alphabetically arranged according to the four MSS-delineated subregions (Regions A, B, C, and D). The sample drawn from each of these regions was based on the disproportionate sampling ratio shown in Table A.1. For the Capital Regional District, all agencies were included and a 60 per cent sample was selected.

Outside the major metropolitan areas, there was a response rate of 88 per cent. In the two major metropolitan areas, including the Fraser Valley, the response rate was 84 per cent. Combining all areas there was a response rate of 85 per cent.

The Questionnaire

Although this study builds upon and extends the pilot survey, there was a substantive shift in the expanded study to examine the effects of contracting out on the non-profit sector. This required a series of new questions, which had to be pre-tested. These questions related to: (1) the relationship between non-profit agencies; (2) the relationship between non-profit agencies and the government; and (3) non-profit agencies' perceptions of the advantages and disadvantages of contracting, the contracting process, standards, and the impact of contracting on a number of agency characteristics. The questionnaire from the pilot survey was revised and pre-tested. Six non-profit agencies in the GVRD participated in the pre-test.

The Interview

The executive director of each agency was sent a letter describing the purpose of the study. An interview was requested so that the questionnaire could be administered. The letter also mentioned that the financial data for the agency, if filled out beforehand, would greatly facilitate the interview.

The interviews in regions outside the two major metropolitan areas were conducted during May and June, 1989. The interviews in the two major metropolitan areas were conducted from August to November of the same year. All interviews were carried out by either the author or a research assistant.

Coding

The challenge in developing the codebook was to ensure that the study captured the richness of the data. The length of the codebook in part reflects the heterogeneity and the diversity of the non-profit sector. The budget data occupies the major portion of the codebook.

The large number of variables listed in the codebook reflects the difficulty in clearly defining what voluntary organizations do. Most voluntary organizations are involved in a blend of activities and provide services to diverse groups. In British Columbia, they may contract to provide services in different program areas with one ministry, or they may contract with several sources to provide services in several different program areas. The coding scheme had to take this into account. For example, in coding how often agencies were required to report on services, the same question had to be coded as many times as there were different ministries or other sources providing contract funding.

The Analysis

The analysis is divided into several parts. Provincial ministry data are analyzed to examine trends in government funding by program area. This is restricted to the Ministry of Social Services because its annual reports present data that can be related to wholly contracted-out program areas. For the ministries of Health and Attorney General, the contracted dollars are embedded within much larger program areas, making it difficult to track funding year to year.

The ministry data are then juxtaposed to data based on the survey of 133 non-profit agencies across the province. Because the survey data are influenced by increased funding from a greater number of sources through time, as well as by an increased number of agencies receiving increased funding from more sources, the analysis presents data for ninety-seven agencies that provided consistent budget data over the seven-year period under study. Funding from the provincial government for these latter agencies is examined in terms of both MSS funding only and funding from all provincial government ministries.

The third part of the analysis examines funding patterns for the ninety-seven agencies in term of the pre- and post-privatization periods. The pre-privatization period includes fiscal years 1982-3, 1983-4, and 1984-5. The post-privatization period covers fiscal years 1985-6, 1986-7, 1987-8, and 1988-9. The pre- and post-privatization data for each agency are based on the mean for each respective period. The tables analyzing the changing bases of government funding present the sum of means over the number of agencies. For nongovernmental funding the same procedure is followed but the ratios are presented instead.

Appendix 2: Tables

Table A.1

Total number of non-profit agencies identified and contacted, total number of interviews completed, and refusal rates by location

Location	# Contacted	# Completed	Refusal rate (%)
100% sampling			
Kamloops	10	9	10.0
Prince George	9	8	11.1
Quesnel	3	3	0.0
Dawson Creek	6	6	0.0
Kelowna	9	7	22.2
Terrace	4	3	25.0
Cranbrook	5	5	0.0
Nelson	5	4	20.0
Nanaimo	9	8	11.1
Subtotal	60	53	11.7
Variable sampling fractions			
GVRD (region A/B)	40	32	20.0
(# identified = 100)			
(.40 sample fraction)			
GVRD (region C)	15	11	26.7
(# identified = 25)			
(.60 sample fraction			
Fraser Valley (D)*	17	17	0.0
(# identified = 28)			
(.60 sample fraction)			
CRD	23	20	13.0
(# identified = 38)			
(.60 sample fraction)			
Subtotal	95	80	15.8
TOTAL	155	133	14.2

* The Fraser Valley (Sumas, Abbotsford, and Matsqui) is included in the large metropolitan area.

Table A.2

Trends in government and nongovernment sources of funding for 133 non-profit agencies (in thousands of dollars, inflation adjusted, 1982 = 100)

Fiscal year	Prov. govt. grants	Prov. govt. contacts	Fed. govt.	Mun. govt.	Total govt. funds
1982-3	22,375	25,330	2,382	626	50,713
1983-4	22,054	26,273	2,136	608	51,071
1984-5	23,371	30,185	2,897	820	57,273
1985-6	22,769	33,541	3,754	780	60,844
1986-7	23,306	43,004	4,910	809	72,029
1987-8	25,313	50,818	5,238	932	82,301
1988-9	24,702	60,209	5,517	933	91,361

Fiscal year	United Way	Earned revenue and fee-for-service	Own fundraising	All nongovt. funds
1982-3	1,422	8,720	3,363	13,505
1983-4	1,486	9,180	3,858	14,524
1984-5	1,576	9,495	3,853	14,924
1985-6	1,633	10,305	4,737	16,675
1986-7	1,771	11,456	5,854	19,081
1987-8	1,780	12,758	6,764	21,302
1988-9	1,933	14,808	7,179	23,920

Table A.3

Summary of annual expenditures by major program classification, MSS, 1982-3 to 1988-9 (in millions of dollars, inflation adjusted, 1982=100)

Fiscal year	GAIN	Rehabilitation and Support[1]	Family and Children's Services[2]	Services to Seniors	Direct Community Services[1]	Admin. and Support	Housing	Pharmacare[2]	Total
1982-3	640.2	132.0	83.9	33.8	90.3	21.4		90.8	1,092.4
1983-4	773.7	134.8	80.3	30.7	89.6	22.2		101.1	1,232.4
1984-5	810.9	139.3	87.3	27.1	87.9	32.0		108.4	1,292.9
1985-6	812.9	135.6	112.0	25.9	62.3	28.6		120.7	1,298.1
1986-7	772.3	128.6	110.6	24.9	65.8	32.0	13.8	140.4	1,288.4
1987-8	755.1	127.4	113.5	27.5	73.5	34.8	13.6		1,145.5
1988-9	755.0	134.6	98.6	228.8	99.9	39.2	15.6		1,171.7

[1] In the *Annual Report*, salaries of line social workers are treated as direct programs costs for 1985-6, 1986-7, and 1987-8. In 1988-9, salaries of line social workers are included under Direct Community Services.

[2] Pharmacare was transferred to the Ministry of Health in 1987-8 and Housing became part of the Ministry of Social Services and Housing in 1986-7.

Source: Ministry of Social Services and Housing, *Annual Reports,* 1980-9

Table A.4

Distribution of different sources of funding for 97 non-profit agencies consistently receiving provincial funding from 1982-3 to 1988-9 (in thousands of dollars, inflation adjusted, 1982=100)

Fiscal year	All govt. funding	Prov. govt. contracts	Prov. govt. grants	Fed. govt.	Mun. govt.
1982-3	32,162	25,330	3,990	2,216	626
1983-4	32,263	26,073	3,709	1,873	608
1984-5	35,220	28,265	3,619	2,521	815
1985-6	37,744	30,790	3,234	2,954	766
1986-7	40,000	32,111	3,400	3,750	755
1987-8	56,822	35,619	3,600	3,419	844
1988-9	64,136	40,858	4,364	3,716	875

Fiscal year	Nongovt. funding	United Way	Earned revenue	Fee-for-service	Own fundraising	Other
1982-3	8,806	1,183	2,915	2,453	1,943	312
1983-4	9,195	1,236	2,846	2,559	2,233	321
1984-5	9,405	1,320	2,580	2,618	2,443	444
1985-6	10,968	1,364	2,649	3,186	3,296	473
1986-7	11,867	1,365	2,784	3,322	3,898	498
1987-8	13,339	1,399	3,444	3,396	4,334	766
1988-9	14,323	1,445	3,476	3,816	4,679	907

Table A.5

Sources of funding and percentage change in sources by type of provincial funding in the pre- and post-privatization periods (in thousands of dollars, inflation adjusted, 1982=100)

	Prov. contract	% change	Prov. grant	% change	Nongovt. funding	% change	Total govt. funding[a]	% change	Total funding	% change	R_1[b]	R_1[c]
Agencies receiving prov. grants (10)												
Pre-privatization	–	–	255	–	439	–	409	–	848	–	0.00	0.52
Post-privatization	–	–	422	+65.4	704	+60.1	598	+46.2	1,302	+53.5	0.00	0.54
Agencies receiving prov. contracts (44)												
Pre-privatization	14,327	–	–	–	4,136	–	15,823	–	19,959	–	1.00	0.21
Post-privatization	18,753	+30.9	–	–	5,722	+38.3	20,434	+29.1	26,146	+31.0	1.00	0.22
Agencies receiving prov. grants and contracts (43)												
Pre-privatization	12,229	–	3,518	–	4,559	–	16,984	–	21,543	–	0.78	0.20
Post-privatization	16,092	+31.6	3,228	–8.2	6,199	+36.0	21,740	+28.0	27,939	+29.7	0.83	0.21

a Government funding includes provincial, federal, and municipal government funding.
b R_1 = provincial government contracts divided by sum of provincial government grants and contracts.
c R_2 = nongovernment funding divided by sum of nongovernment and government funding.

Table A.6

Sources of funding and percentage change in sources, by type of provincial funding and by its pre- and post-privatization increase or decrease (in thousands of dollars, inflation adjusted, 1982=100)

	Prov. contract	% change	Prov. grant	% change	Nongovt. funding	% change	Total govt. funding[a]	% change	Total funding	% change	R_1[b]	R_2[c]
Agencies receiving prov. grants (10)												
Grant funding increase (4)												
Pre-privatization	–	–	71	–	39	–	114	–	153	–	0.00	0.25
Post-privatization	–	–	310	+337.5	120	+207.7	364	+220.2	484	+216.3	0.00	0.25
Grant funding decrease (6)												
Pre-privatization	–	–	184	–	401	–	295	–	696	–	0.00	0.58
Post-privatization	–	–	111	–39.5	584	+45.7	234	–20.9	818	+17.5	0.00	0.71
Agencies receiving prov. grants (44)												
Contract funding increase (37)												
Pre-privatization	11,988	–	–	–	3,614	–	13,359	–	16,973	–	1.00	0.21
Post-privatization	16,889	+40.9	–	–	4,992	+38.1	18,454	+33.1	23,446	+38.1	1.00	0.21

(continued on next page)

Table A.6 (continued)

	Prov. contract	% change	Prov. grant	% change	Nongovt. funding	% change	Total govt. funding[a]	% change	Total funding	% change	R₁[b]	R₂[c]
Contract funding decrease (7)												
Pre-privatization	2,339	–	–	–	522	–	2,464	–	2,986	–	1.00	0.17
Post-privatization	1,864	–20.3	–	–	730	+39.8	1,969	–20.1	2,699	–9.6	1.00	0.27
Agencies receiving prov. grants and contracts (43)												
Contracts>grants (24)												
Pre-privatization	11,584	–	540	–	3,202	–	12,272	–	15,929	–	0.96	0.20
Post-privatization	14,948	+29.0	575	+6.5	4,377	–	16,534	+29.9	20,911	+31.3	0.96	0.21
Grants>contracts (14)												
Pre-privatization	48	–	2,116	–	1,021	–	2,550	–	3,571	–	0.02	0.29
Post-privatization	240	+400	2,040	–3.6	1,249	+22.3	3,393	+29.1	4,542	+27.2	0.11	0.28
Grants switched to contracts (5)												
Pre-privatization	597	–	861	–	335	–	1,707	–	2,042	–	0.41	0.17
Post-privatization	904	+51.4	613	–28.8	573	+71.0	1,912	+12.0	2,485	+21.7	0.60	0.23

[a] Government funding includes federal, provincial, and municipal government funding.
[b] R_1 = provincial government contracts divided by sum of provincial government grants and contracts.
[c] R_2 = nongovernmental funding divided by sum of nongovernment and government funding.

Table A.7

Number and percentage of non-profit agencies receiving provincial grants and/or contracts

	# of agencies	% of sample
Agencies receiving prov. grants only	11	8.3[a]
Agencies receiving prov. contracts only	44	33.1
Agencies receiving prov. grants and contracts	45	33.8[b]
Agencies with missing budgets	14	10.5
Agencies starting in mid- or late 1980s and missing pre- or post-privatization data	19	14.3

[a] The YMCA is excluded from the analysis. The number of agencies belonging to this category is 10 for subsequent analysis.

[b] Glendale Lodge and the Greater Vancouver Mental Health Association are excluded from the analysis. The number of agencies belonging to this category is 43 for subsequent analysis.

Table A.8

Proportion of different sources of nongovernment funding, by type of provincial funding and by its pre- and post-privatization increase or decrease

	United Way	Earned revenue	Fee-for-service	Own fundraising	Other
Agencies receiving prov. grants					
Grant funding increase (5)	25%	5%	3%	53%	13%
Pre-privatization	28	2	1	54	14
Post-privatization	24	6	4	53	13
Grant funding decrease (5)	32	3	1	62	2
Pre-privatization	38	3	1	57	1
Post-privatization	29	3	1	64	2
Agencies receiving prov. contracts (44)					
Contract increase (40)	14	18	32	29	7
Pre-privatization	17	18	37	23	5
Post-privatization	13	18	29	32	8
Contract decrease (4)	3	32	45	18	2
Pre-privatization	3	38	40	17	2
Post-privatization	2	30	47	18	2

Agencies receiving prov. grants and contracts (43)

Government contracts>government grants (24)	5	44	25	23	3
Pre-privatization	6	47	24	21	2
Post-privatization	5	43	25	24	3
Government grants>government contracts (14)	18	16	23	38	5
Pre-privatization	17	38	11	29	5
Post-privatization	18	4	29	43	5
Government grants switched to contracts (5)	13	8	31	44	4
Pre-privatization	18	10	35	27	10
Post-privatization	11	7	29	51	2

Table A.9

Proportion of different sources of nongovernment funding, by type of provincial funding and by its pre- and post-privatization increase or decrease

	Govt. funding[1]	Nongovt. funding	Private and charitable giving[2]	Earned revenue and fee-for-service[3]
	Total funding	Total funding	Nongovt. funding	Nongovt. funding
Agencies receiving prov. grants (10)				
Grant funding increase (4)				
Pre-privatization	75%	25%	82%	18%
Post-privatization	75	25	77	23
Grant funding decrease (6)				
Pre-privatization	42	58	95	5
Post-privatization	29	71	93	7
Agencies receiving prov. contracts (44)				
Contract funding increase (37)				
Pre-privatization	79	21	40	60
Post-privatization	79	21	45	55
Contract funding decrease (7)				
Pre-privatization	83	17	20	80
Post-privatization	73	27	21	79

Agencies receiving prov. grants and contracts (43)

Contracts>grants (24)				
Pre-privatization	80	20	27	73
Post-privatization	79	21	29	71
Grants>contracts (14)				
Pre-privatization	71	29	46	54
Post-privatization	73	27	62	38
Grants switched to contracts (5)				
Pre-privatization	84	16	46	54
Post-privatization	77	23	62	38

[1] Includes funding from federal, provincial, and municipal governments.
[2] Includes United Way, donations, membership, fundraising from gaming, etc.
[3] Includes fee-for-service and other business charges.

Notes

Chapter 1: New Thinking on the Voluntary Sector

1 For the history of the welfare state in Canada see Guest (1986) and Banting (1987a).

2 The residual model implies that state responsibility for its citizens begins only when the family or market fails. It is therefore limited to marginal groups in society. The institutional model is universalistic – applying to the entire population – and incorporates an institutional commitment to welfare.

3 Mishra (1977) uses the term corporatist differently. He sees corporatism as an approach to welfare that does not reject the mixed economy and the welfare state. The major economic players (capital and labour) recognize their interdependence and the need to negotiate on issues of productivity, wages, employment policy, and social welfare. Consensus is arrived at through bipartite or tripartite agreements between business, labour, and governments. In this context, Scandinavia is usually classified as having a corporatist approach to welfare.

4 Public policies encourage the development of the private sector. The public sector caters to those who fail in the market: the working class and the poor.

5 The Co-operative Commonwealth Federation later became the New Democratic Party.

6 'Keynesianism' refers to a set of social and economic policies designed to overcome the crisis of the Depression. The Depression resulted from a failure of consumption levels to keep pace with the output generated by mass production. Keynes argued that during economic upswings governments should tax heavily in order to put aside money to be spent on job creation projects during recessions. This strategy would stimulate consumer demand, which would in turn stimulate economic growth.

7 Corporate tax revenues falling short of expectations is recognized as one of the factors contributing to this country's deficit, which has grown steadily since the 1950s. Large corporations have been able to avoid or defer paying taxes through exemptions, concessions, and deferrals. The shortfall in revenue forces the government to borrow in order to finance its spending, thereby increasing the deficit. Other factors contributing to the deficit

growth are high interest rates on money borrowed by government, high social expenditures caused by severe recessions as in the early 1980s, and, according to Swankey (1985), the military budget.

8 This 5 per cent cap was first announced for 1990-1 and 1991-2, and then extended to cover an additional three years, to 1994-5.

9 The National Council of Welfare, in 'A Statement by the National Council of Welfare on the 1991 Federal Budget Speech' (1991), estimated that these freezes would lead to a total disappearance of the federal cash contribution in some provinces by 1996-7, and everywhere by 2007-8.

10 Community Panel, Family and Children's Services, 1992. *Making Changes, A Place to Start.* Report of the Community Panel, Family and Children's Services Legislative Review in British Columbia; Community Panel, Family and Children's Services, 1992. *Liberating Our Children, Liberating Our Nation.* Report of the Aboriginal Committee, Community Panel, Family and Children's Services Legislation Review in British Columbia.

11 The terms 'New Right' and 'neoconservative' are used interchangeably. Neoconservatives, however, are less extreme than the New Right in their attitude toward the role of the state.

Chapter 2: Voluntary Sector-Government Collaboration in BC

1 Much of the 19 per cent increase in the Ministry of Social Services and Housing expenditure in 1983-4 could be attributed to the increase in Income Assistance and Guaranteed Annual Income for Need (GAIN) expenditure for handicapped people, rather than to other programs.

2 This program allowed individuals on social assistance to receive a small remuneration from MSS if they performed volunteer work in the community.

3 Bureaucratic disentitlement refers to the practice of disentitling recipients to benefits based on decisions made in government. Thus, for example, if there is no legislative mandate defining who can qualify for subsidies, certain groups can become disentitled if government decides to specify income levels above which subsidies do not apply.

4 For the history and evolution of the public welfare system from Confederation to 1982 in British Columbia see Clague et al. (1984).

5 The Seebohm Report, U.K. (1968) advocated centralization of social and health services for administrative purposes and decentralization for delivery purposes.

6 The CELDIC Report, Canada (1970) stressed the need for 'a range of services that is economically, geographically and socially acceptable to the child in need and to those responsible for his day-to-day care.' It also advocated co-ordinated efforts to serve the needs of the 'whole child.'

7 The Castonguay-Nepveu Report, Quebec (1976) dealt with health care and social services in Quebec. It called for the establishment of a single ministry to coordinate a decentralized, differentiated health and social services system at regional and local levels. It also called for local participation in the operation of health and social service centres.

8 The Hastings Report, Canada (1972) recommended the establishment of community health centres, after finding that consumers in group practice received better value for their money.

Chapter 3: Changing Relationship

1 During the Social Credit era this ministry was known as the Ministry of Social Services and Housing. In 1991 it became the Ministry of Social Services and is referred to as such throughout the book.

2 See Appendix 1 for methodology.

3 Recent data generated for the Korbin Commission in 1993 show that in fiscal year 1991-2 the provincial government spent approximately $630 million in community human services. Seventy-five per cent of this expenditure belonged to MSS. The money was allocated in the following way: approximately $500 million in direct contracts with staffed agencies, operated by non-profit, proprietary, government, and the public sector; $70 million in contracts with individuals who did not hire staff; and $60 million in third-party transfers, in which money was transferred to individuals who then used it to pay for services provided by staffed agencies or individuals, for example, day care. $440 million of the $500 million spent in direct contracts with staffed agencies went to non-profit agencies. This figure is probably an underestimate because the survey included only those agencies (non-profit, incorporated business or company, or a self-employed individual who also employs staff) receiving $20,000 or more from the government.

4 In 1988 the Ministry of the Solicitor General was established. This newly established ministry took over some of the responsibilities that had previously come under the Ministry of the Attorney General. In 1991, under the newly elected NDP government, the two ministries were amalgamated again under the Ministry of the Attorney General.

5 The information in the previous two paragraphs was obtained from the annual reports issued by each of the three ministries as well as personal communication with the respective executive offices in each ministry. It should be noted that annual reports are generally issued one to two years after the year to which they refer. In 1993 the most current annual reports relate to 1991-2.

6 The trend lines are based on expenditure estimates provided in BC Ministry of Finance, *Public Accounts of British Columbia,* from 1982-3 to 1988-9. This publication was preferred because expenditure items were categorized much more consistently than in the annual reports published by MSS.

7 Family and Children's Services is an official program within MSS targeting families and children. In the context of this book, services to families and children is used more generically than it is under MSS programs. Services targeting these groups are also funded by other ministries as well as through the agencies' own fundraising.

8 Services to mentally handicapped persons, whose needs cannot be met in their communities, have been provided by these three institutions: Glendale, serving Vancouver Island; Tranquille, formerly serving the interior of the province; and Woodlands, serving the Lower Mainland and the north coast.

9 Includes ministry-operated residential care, social services, and training for the physically and mentally handicapped, as well as grants and contributions for these services and for the community-based services and day care. It also provides for rental and maintenance of facilities for handicapped persons.

10 Tranquille, located in Kamloops, provided residential assessment and training services for mentally handicapped children and adults from the northern and interior regions of the province. It was closed 31 December 1984.

11 Woodlands is expected to close in 1995.

12 Glendale Lodge was privatized and transferred to a non-profit society in 1987-8. Provincial government funding received by Glendale Lodge was obtained from the survey data.

13 The total aggregate expenditures on these program areas have not been included because of the difference in scale that could not be accommodated in this figure.

14 Personal communication with a MSS research officer indicated that it would require considerable work to assemble the kind of database that would answer these research questions.

15 Expenditure divided by the provincial population.

16 The large metropolitan communities were represented by the Victoria Capital Regional District (CRD) and the Greater Vancouver Regional District (GVRD), as well as Matsqui, Sumas, and Abbotsford, suburban communities that abut the GVRD. The medium-sized communities were represented by Prince George, Kelowna, Kamloops, and Nanaimo. Cranbrook, Nelson, Dawson Creek, Quesnel, and Terrace represented the small communities.

17 The pre-privatization data were based on the fiscal years 1982-3, 1983-4, and 1984-5. The post-privatization period data were based on fiscal years 1985-6 to 1988-9 inclusive.

18 To compare changes in different funding sources, the funding was aggregated into the pre- and post-privatization totals. The mean for the pre- and post-privatization periods was then calculated by dividing these totals by the number of years of pre-privatization (1982-3, 1983-4, 1984-5) and post-privatization (1985-6, 1986-7, 1987-8, 1988-9). This number divided by the number of agencies gives us the mean for each agency.

19 Fourteen of the agencies did not provide budget data and another nineteen started in the mid- or late 1980s. These agencies were excluded because it was not possible to calculate the pre- and post-privatization data. Another three very large agencies receiving 100 per cent funding from government sources were excluded because they skewed the data. Thus, this analysis is limited to 97 agencies.

20 For agencies that received either grants or contracts from the provincial government, the disaggregation is based on whether these sources of funding were increasing or decreasing. For agencies that received both grants and contracts, disaggregation by increases and decreases in each source of funding would lead to too many categories. Groupings for agencies receiving both forms of funding were therefore based on whether contracts were larger than grants or grants were larger than contracts, and whether agencies switched from grant to contract funding between the pre- and post-privatization periods.

21 The 1993 Korbin Report shows that in 1991-2 there were approximately 1,800 agencies that received funds in excess of $20,000 for community-contracted services from the following provincial ministries: MSS, Health,

Attorney General, Education, and Women's Equality. This number includes non-profit societies, incorporated businesses or companies, or self-employed individuals who also employ staff. Seventy per cent of these agencies are non-profit, 20 per cent are registered companies, 8 per cent are self-employed individuals with staff, and 2 per cent are self-employed with no staff.

22 See Appendix 1 for more specific description of study areas.

23 The 1993 Korbin Report estimated that in 1991-2, 914 (51.8 per cent) of the 1764 agencies delivering community contracted services received payments between $20,000 and $99,999; 659 (37.4 per cent) received between $100,000 and $499,999; 96 (5.4 per cent) received between $500,000 and $999,999; and 95 (5.4 per cent) received $1 million plus. The 191 agencies receiving $500,000 or more in 1991/2 represented only 10 per cent of all agencies but captured 60 per cent of contracted dollars. In contrast, the 914 agencies (51.8 per cent) in the $20,000 to $99,999 range captured 10 per cent of total contract dollars.

24 According to the Korbin Report (1993) the $628 million spent by the provincial government on contracted community services was allocated to the following services: residential mental handicapped services (20 per cent), mental handicap training and support (8 per cent), child, youth, and family support services (12 per cent), children's care, residential (18 per cent), child day care (13 per cent), employment initiative (8 per cent), alcohol and drug programs (5 per cent), adult mental handicap services (6 per cent), victim assistance and family violence (3 per cent), adult day care (1 per cent), correctional services (3 per cent), and other (3 per cent).

Chapter 4: Evolving 'Partnership'

1 The technical report for the Contracted Community Social Sector provides specific data showing how wages vary even for similar jobs within a sector.

2 Under the Canada Assistance Plan, 50 per cent of provincial outlays for children and families qualifying under the income test are cost shared by the federal government. Under Bill C-69, a 5 per cent cap on the Canada Assistance Plan was extended through to 1994-5 to the 'have' provinces of Ontario, Alberta, and BC. Krashinsky (1986) also shows that while Nova Scotia and Saskatchewan only subsidize day-care spaces in non-profit organizations, British Columbia is among those provinces that subsidize spaces in both for-profit and non-profit organizations.

3 This data is from another table not included here because of its brevity and because internal standards of service referred to the list covered in Table 4.4.

Chapter 5: Autonomy of the Voluntary Sector

1 Sixty-three of the 133 non-profit societies reported revenues from fee-for-service and other charges in the fiscal year 1988-9.

2 The material on Revenue Canada Interpretation Bulletin IT-496 is from Krashinsky (1986).

Bibliography

Abramovitz, M. 1986. The Privatization of the Welfare State: A Review. *Social Work* 31, 4 (July-Aug.):257-64

Ascher, K. 1987. *The Politics of Privatization: Contracting Out Public Services.* Basingstoke: Macmillan

Austin, M.J. 1984. Managing Cutbacks in the 1980s. *Social Work* 29(5):428-34

Bacon, R. and W. Eltis. 1976. *Britain's Economic Problems: Too Few Producers.* London: Macmillan

Banting, K.G. 1987a. *The Welfare State and Canadian Federalism.* Kingston and Montreal: McGill-Queen's University Press

– 1987b. The Welfare State and Inequality in the 1980s. *Canadian Review of Sociology and Anthropology* 24 (3):309-38

Basoff, B.Z. 1982. The Community Clinics, Will They Survive? *Social Work in Health Care* 8, 1 (Fall):71-9

Battle, K. and Sherri Torjman. 1993. *Federal Social Programs: Setting the Record Straight.* Ottawa: Caledon Institute of Social Policy

BC. See British Columbia

Beck, Bertram M. 1970. The Voluntary Social Welfare Agency: A Reassessment. *Social Service Review* 44, 2 (June):147-54

– 1971. Government Contracts with Non-Profit Social Welfare Corporations. In *The Dilemma of Accountability in Modern Government: Independence versus Control,* edited by B.L.R. Smith and D.C. Hague, 213-29. New York: St. Martin's Press

Beresford, P. and S. Croft. 1984. Welfare Pluralism: The New Face of Fabianism. *Critical Social Policy* 9:19-39

Berger, P.L. and R.J. Neuhaus. 1977. *To Empower People: The Role of Mediating Structures in Public Policy.* Washington, DC: American Enterprise Institute for Public Policy Research

Best, R.L. 1960. Improving Productivity in the Government Sector: The Role of Contracting Out. In *Responses to Economic Change,* edited by D. Laider, 203-95. Toronto: University of Toronto Press

Beveridge, L.W. 1984. *Voluntary Action: A Report on Methods of Social Advance.* London: George Allen and Unwin

Board of Directors of Little Mountain Neighbourhood House. 1984. *Brief to the Ministry of Human Resources.* Vancouver: Board of Directors, Little Mountain Neighbourhood House

Bosanquet, N. 1983. *After the New Right.* London: Heinemann

Bracken, D. and P. Hudson. 1987. *Privatization and Social Welfare: The Manitoba Experience.* Winnipeg: Child and Family Services Research Group, School of Social Work, University of Manitoba

Branch, L.G. 1980. Functional Abilities of the Elderly: An Update on the Massachusetts Health Care Panel Study. In *Epidemiology of Aging,* edited by S.G. Haynes and M. Feinleib. NIH Publications no. 80-969. Washington, DC: U.S. Government Printing Office

Brenton, M. 1982. Changing Relationships in Dutch Social Services. *Journal of Social Policy* 11 (1):59-80

– 1985. *The Voluntary Sector in British Social Services.* London: Longman

Brilliant, E.L. 1973. Private or Public: A Model of Ambiguities. *Social Service Review* 47, 3 (Sept.):384-96

British Columbia Government Employees' Union. 1985. *A Promise Broken – The Effects of Restraint on Delivery of Social Services in British Columbia.* Burnaby, BC: BCGEU

British Columbia Ministry of Finance. 1983 to 1985a (annual publication). *B.C. Budget.* Victoria: Ministry of Finance

– 1980 to 1985b (annual publication). *Estimates.* Victoria: Ministry of Finance

– 1982 to 1985 (annual publication). *Public Accounts of British Columbia.* Victoria: Ministry of Finance

British Columbia Ministry of Finance and Corporate Relations. 1986 to 1987a (annual publication). *B.C. Budget.* Victoria: Ministry of Finance and Corporate Relations

– 1986 to 1987b (annual publication). *Estimates.* Victoria: Ministry of Finance and Corporate Relations

– 1986 to 1989 (annual publication). *Public Accounts of British Columbia.* Victoria: Ministry of Finance and Corporate Relations

British Columbia Ministry of Human Resources. 1974 to 1975 (annual publication). *Annual Reports.* Victoria: Ministry of Human Resources

British Columbia Ministry of Social Services and Housing. 1980 to 1989 (annual publication). *Annual Reports.* Victoria: Ministry of Social Services and Housing

Brooks, N. 1987. *The Quest for Tax Reforms.* Toronto: Carswell Press

Burd, R.P. and J.B. Richmond. 1979. Public and Private Sector: A Developing Partnership in Human Services. *American Journal of Orthopsychiatry* 49 (April):218-29

Caledon Institute of Social Policy. 1992. *Child Benefit Primer: A Response to the Government Proposal.* Ottawa: The Institute

Callahan, M. and C. McNiven. 1988. British Columbia. In *Privatization and Provincial Social Services in Canada,* edited by J.S. Ismail and Y. Vaillancourt, 13-39. Edmonton: University of Alberta Press

Caner, E. 1986. Four Years of Cutbacks: B.C. Has Been a Testing Ground for the Policies of Restraint. *The Facts* (May-June):48-51

Castonguay-Nepveu Report. See Quebec Commission of Inquiry on Health and Social Welfare

CELDIC. See Commission on Emotional and Learning Disabilities in Children

Chorney, H. 1986. The Deficit – The Spurious Need to Reduce the Deficit Serves as an Excuse for Cutting Service. *The Facts* (May-June):6-10

City of Prince George, Social Advisory Committee. 1986. *Report to City Council on Social Services*. Prince George, BC: City of Prince George

Clague, M., R. Dill, R. Seebaran, and B. Wharf. 1984. *Reforming Human Services: The Experience of the Community Resource Boards in B.C.* Vancouver: UBC Press

Commission on Emotional and Learning Disabilities in Children (CELDIC). 1970. *One Million Children*. Toronto: Leonard Crainford

Community Council of Greater Victoria. 1986. *Social Need and Social Service Provision in Greater Victoria*. Planning and Information Exchange Report no. 4. Victoria: CCGV

Community Health Centre Project Committee. 1972. *The Community Health Centre in Canada*. (The Hastings Report). Ottawa: Information Canada

Community Panel, Family and Children's Services. 1992. *Liberating Our Children: Liberating Our Nation*. Report of the Aboriginal Committee, Community Panel, Family and Children's Services Legislation Review in BC

– 1992. *Making Changes: A Place to Start*. Report of the Community Panel, Family and Children's Services Legislative Review in BC

Crimmins, J.C. and M. Keil. 1983. *Enterprise in the Nonprofit Sector*. Washington, DC: Partners for Liveable Places, Washington, DC, and the Rockefeller Brothers Fund, New York

Culpitt, I. 1989. *Welfare and Citizenship: Beyond the Crisis of the Welfare State*. London: Sage Publications

Currie, Janet and Fred Pishalski. 1983. Loosening the Fabric: The Termination of the Family Support Worker Program in British Columbia. Mimeo

Davies, L. and E. Shragge, eds. 1990. *Bureaucracy and Community*. Montreal: Black Rose Books

DeHoog, Ruth Hoogland. 1984. *Contracting Out for Human Services, Economic, Political and Organizational Perspective*. Albany: State University of New York Press

Demone, H.W. and M. Gibelman. 1984. Reaganomics: Its Impact on the Voluntary Not-For-Profit Sector. *Social Work* (Sept.-Oct.):421-7

Doern, G.B. 1987. The Tories and the Crown: Restraining and Privatizing in a Political Minefield. In *How Ottawa Spends 1987/88: Restraining the State*, edited by M.J. Prince, 129-75. Toronto: Methuen

Donaldson, David. 1985. *On the Provision of Public Services by the Voluntary Sector*. Vancouver: BC Economic Policy Institute, University of British Columbia

Douglas, J. 1983. *Why Charity? The Case for a Third Sector*. Beverly Hills: Sage

Drucker, P.F. 1969. *The Age of Discontinuity: Guidelines to our Changing Society*. New York: Harper and Row

Dunn, Denis E. 1980a. *Commentary and Recommendations Relevant to Emerging Social Service Needs in British Columbia*. Vancouver: United Way/SPARC Joint Committee

– 1980b. *An Historical and Contemporary Review of the Financing of Social Services in British Columbia, Illustrating the Roles of the Private and Public Sectors in Funding and Delivering These Services*. Vancouver: United Way/SPARC Joint Committee

– 1980c. *Public Funding Policies and Procedures in British Columbia: A Summary of Specific Problems Experienced by Voluntary Agencies in the Social Services Sector*. Vancouver: United Way/SPARC Joint Committee

Eisenstadt, S.N. and Ora Ahimeir, eds. 1985. *The Welfare State and Its Aftermath*. London: Croom Helm

Epp, E.A. 1989. Thinking the Unthinkable: The Fair Taxation of Corporations. *Canadian Review of Social Policy* 24 (Nov.):6-7

Esping-Andersen, G. 1985. Power and Distributional Regimes. *Politics and Society* 14 (2):223-56

– 1987. Citizenship and Socialism: De-Commodification and Solidarity in the Welfare State. In *Stagnation and Renewal*, edited by G. Esping-Andersen, M. Rein, and Lee Rainwater, Armonk, NY: M.E. Sharpe

– 1989. The Three Political Economies of the Welfare State. *Canadian Review of Sociology and Anthropology* 26 (1):10-14

Ewalt, P.L. and M. Cohen. 1975. Total Agency Issues and the Short Term Grant. *Social Casework* 56 (June):334-42

Faid, P. 1985. Privatization: Eroding the Social Safety Net. *Perception* 9, 2 (Nov.-Dec.):8-11

Ferris, J.M. and Elizabeth Graddy. 1989. Fading Distinctions among the Nonprofit, Government and For-Profit Sectors. In *The Future of the Nonprofit Sector*, edited by V.A. Hodgkinson, R.W. Lyman, and Associates, 123-39. San Francisco: Jossey-Bass

Filer, J.H. 1975. *Giving in America: Toward a Stronger Voluntary Sector*. Report of the Commission on Private Philanthropy and Public Needs. Washington, DC: Commission on Private Philanthropy and Public Needs

Flora, P. and A.J. Heidenheimer, eds. *The Development of Welfare States in Europe and America*. New Brunswick: Transaction Books

François, Houle. 1983. Economic Strategy and Restructuring of the Fordist-Wage-Labour Relationship in Canada. *Studies in Political Economy* 11:127-49

Freila, C. 1986. Privatization and Commercialization. In *A New Era For Voluntarism*, Proceedings of a conference held in Toronto, 1-3 June 1986, 46-55. Toronto: United Way of Greater Toronto

Friedman, M. 1962. *Capitalism and Freedom*. Chicago: University of Chicago Press

Friedman, M. and R. Friedman. 1980. *Free to Choose*. Harmondsworth: Penguin Books

Gamble, A. 1979. The Free Economy and the Strong State. *Socialist Register*:1-25. London: Merlin Press; New York: Monthly Review Press

George, V. and P. Wilding. 1976. *Ideology and Social Welfare*. London: Routledge and Kegan Paul

– 1984. *The Impact of Social Policy*. London: Routledge and Kegan Paul

Gibelman, M. 1981. Are Clients Better Served When Services Are Purchased? *Public Welfare* 39 (4):27-33

Gideon, R. and W. Schworm. 1984. *Does B.C. Need Fiscal Restraint?* Vancouver: BC Economic Policy Institute, University of British Columbia

Gilbert, N. 1977. Transformation of Social Services. *Social Service Review* 51 (Dec.):624-41
– 1983. *Capitalism and the Welfare State: Dilemmas of Social Benevolence.* New Haven: Yale University Press
– 1984. Welfare for Profit: Moral, Empirical and Theoretical Perspectives. *Journal of Social Policy* 13 (1):64-74
Gladstone, F. 1979. *Voluntary Action in a Changing World.* London: Bedford Square Press
Glazer, Nathan. 1983. Toward a Self-Service Society. *The Public Interest* 70 (Winter):63-90
Glennerster, H. 1983. *The Future of the Welfare State.* London: Heinemann
Goetchens, Vernon M. 1983. Voluntarism ... and Reagan. *Journal of the Institute for Socioeconomic Studies* 9 (Summer):36-48
Golding, P. 1983. Rethinking Common Sense about Social Policy. In *Thatcherism and the Poor,* edited by D. Bull and P. Wilding, (n.p.). London: Child Poverty Action Group
Gough, I. 1979. *The Political Economy of the Welfare State.* London: Macmillan
– 1980. Thatcherism and the Welfare State. *Marxism Today* (July):7-12
Guest, D. 1986. *The Emergence of Social Security in Canada.* Vancouver: UBC Press
Hadley, R. and S. Hatch. 1981. *Social Welfare and the Failure of the State.* London: Allen and Unwin
Hadley, R. and M. McGrath. 1980. *Going Local: Neighbourhood Social Services.* London: Bedford Square Press
Hall, P.D. 1987. Abandoning the Rhetoric of Independence: Reflections on the Nonprofit Sector in the Post Liberal Era. *Journal of Voluntary Action Research* 16 (1 & 2):11-28
Hansmann, H. 1980. The Role of Nonprofit Enterprise. *Yale Law Journal* 89:835-901
– 1987. Economic Theories of Nonprofit Organization. In *The Nonprofit Sector: A Research Handbook,* edited by W.W. Powell, 27-42. New Haven, CT: Yale University Press
– 1989. The Two Nonprofit Sectors: Fee for Service versus Donative Organizations. In *The Future of the Nonprofit Sector,* edited by V.A. Hodgkinson, R.W. Lyman, and Associates, 91-102. San Francisco: Jossey-Bass
Hastings Report. See Community Health Centre Project Committee
Hatch, S. 1979. The Wolfenden Report on Voluntary Organizations. In *The Yearbook of Social Policy,* edited by M. Brown and S. Baldwin, 101-12. London: Routledge and Kegan Paul
– 1980. *Outside the State.* London: Croom Helm
– 1981. The Voluntary Sector, A Larger Role? In *A New Look at the Personal Social Services,* edited by E.M. Goldberg and S. Hatch, 68-78. London: Policy Studies Institute
Hatch, S. and I. Mocroft. 1983. *Components of Welfare.* London: Bedford Square Press
Hayek, F.A. 1944. *The Road to Serfdom.* London: Routledge and Kegan Paul
Heclo, H. and A. Wildavsky. 1981. *The Private Government of Public Money.* London: Macmillan

Heidemheimer, A.J., H. Heclo, and C.T. Adams. 1983. *Comparative Public Policy: The Politics of Social Choice in Europe and America.* New York: St. Martin's Press

Higgins, J. 1978. *The Poverty Business.* Oxford: Blackwell and Robertson

Hodgkinson, V.A., Richard W. Lyman, and Associates. 1989. *The Future of the Nonprofit Sector.* San Francisco: Jossey-Bass

Hollingsworth, J.R. and E.J. Hollingsworth. 1986. A Comparison of Non-Profit, For-Profit and Public Hospitals in the US: 1935 to the Present. Working Paper no. 113. Program on Non-Profit Organizations, Institute for Social and Policy Studies, Yale University

Howlett M. and K. Brownsey. 1988. The Old Reality and The New Reality: Party Politics and Public Policy in B.C. 1941-1987. *Studies in Political Economy* 25 (Spring):141-75

Hurl, L.F. 1984. Privatized Social Service Systems: Lessons from Ontario Children's Services. *Canadian Public Policy* 10 (4):395-425

– 1986a. Privatization of Social Services: Time to Move the Debate Along. *Canadian Public Policy* 12 (3):507-12

– 1986b. Keeping on Top of Government Contracting: The Challenge to Social Work Educators. *Journal of Social Work Education* 22 (2):6-18

Hurl, L.F. and D.J. Tucker. 1986. Limitations of an Act of Faith: An Analysis of the MacDonald Commission's Stance on Social Services. *Canadian Public Policy* 12:606-21

Ismail, J.S. and Yves Vaillancourt. 1988. *Privatization and Provincial Social Services in Canada: Policy Administration and Service Delivery.* Edmonton: University of Alberta Press

James, E. 1983. How Nonprofits Grow: A Model. *Journal of Policy Analysis and Management* 2 (3):350-3

Jenson, J. 1989. 'Different' but not 'Exceptional': Canada's Permeable Fordism. *Canadian Review of Sociology and Anthropology* 26 (1):69-93

Johnson, N. 1981. *Voluntary Social Services.* Oxford: Blackwell

– 1987. *The Welfare State in Transition.* London: Wheatsheaf Books

– 1989. The Privatization of Welfare. *Social Policy and Administration* 23:17-30

Judge, K. 1982. The Public Purchase of Social Care: British Confirmation of the American Experience. *Policy and Politics* 10 (4):397-416

Kamerman, Sheila. 1983. The Mixed Economy of Welfare: Public and Private. *Social Work* 28, 1 (Jan.-Feb.):5-10

Kamerman, S.B. and A.J. Kahn. 1989. *Privatization and the Welfare State.* Princeton, NJ: Princeton University Press

Kesselman, R.M. 1979. Public Fiscal Policy and Voluntary Agencies in Welfare States. *Social Service Review* 53 (March) 1-14

Kitchen, H.M. 1976. A Statistical Estimation of the Operation Cost Function for Municipal Refuse Collection. *Public Finance Quarterly* 4 (Jan.):57-76

Korbin Report. Report of the Commission of Inquiry into the Public Service and Public Sector. 1993. *The Public Service in British Columbia*, Vol. 1; *The Public Service in British Columbia*, Vol. 2. Victoria: Crown Publications

Klein, R., ed. 1974. *Inflation and Priorities.* London: Centre for Studies in Social Policy

Klein, R.M. and M. O'Higgins, ed. 1984. *The Future of Welfare.* Oxford: Blackwell

Kramer, R.M. 1979. Public Fiscal Policy and Voluntary Agencies in Welfare States. *Social Service Review* 53 (March):1-14
– 1981. *Voluntary Agencies in the Welfare State.* Berkeley: University of California Press
– 1985. The Future of the Voluntary Agency in a Mixed Economy. *Journal of Applied Behavioural Science* 21 (4):377-91
– 1986. Voluntary Agencies and the Personal Social Services. In *The Nonprofit Sector: A Research Handbook,* edited by Walter W. Powell, 240-57. New Haven: Yale University Press
Krashinsky, M. 1977. *Day Care as a Public Policy in Ontario.* Toronto: Ontario Economic Council
– 1986. *An Exploratory Review of Selected Issues in For-Profit Versus Not-for-Profit Child Care.* Toronto: SPR Associates
Kristol, I. 1983. *Reflections of a Neoconservative.* New York: Basic Books
Langford, J.W. 1983. The Question of Quangos: Quasi-Public Services Agencies in British Columbia. *Canadian Public Administration* 26 (Fall):563-76
Lanning, H. 1981. *Government and Voluntary Sector in the U.S.A.* London: National Council for Voluntary Organizations
Lawrence, R. 1983. Voluntary Action: A Stalking Horse for the Right. *Critical Social Policy* 2, 3 (Spring):14-30
Lazar, F. 1986. The Public Sector – A Strong Case Can Be Made for Maintaining Public Services. *The Facts* (May-June):2-5
LeGrand, J. 1982. *The Strategy of Equality.* London: Allen and Unwin
LeGrand, J. and R. Robinson, eds. 1984. *Privatization and the Welfare State.* London: Allen and Unwin
Levens, B.R. and Kay Melliship. 1986. *Regaining Dignity: An Examination of the Cost of Basic Living in the Lower Mainland; the Adequacy of Income Assistance (GAIN) Rates, in December 1985.* Vancouver: Social Planning and Research Council of BC
Lifset, Reid. 1989. Cash Cows or Sacred Cows: The Politics of the Commercialization Movement. In *The Future of the Nonprofit Sector,* edited by V.A. Hodgkinson, R.W. Lyman, and Associates, 140-67. San Francisco: Jossey-Bass
Lipsky, M. 1984. Bureaucratic Disentitlement in Social Welfare Programs. *Social Service Review* 58 (1):4-27
Lipsky, M. and S.R. Smith. 1990. Nonprofit Organizatins, Government and their Welfare State. *Political Science Quarterly* 104 (4):625-48
Lipsky, M. and M.A. Thibodeau. 1988. Feeding the Hungry with Surplus Commodities. *Political Science Quarterly* 103 (2):223-24
McAfee, R.P. and John McMillan. 1986. *Incentives in Government Contracting.* Toronto: Ontario Economic Council
McDavid, James. 1984. *Residential Solid Waste Collection in Canadian Municipalities.* Victoria: School of Public Administration, University of Victoria
Macdonald, J.A. 1984. Privatization and Social Services in B.C. – An Examination of the Issues in Legal and Historical Perspective. Vancouver: School of Social Work, University of British Columbia. Mimeo
MacKinnon, F. 1973. Changing Patterns in Public-Voluntary Relationships in Canada. *Child Welfare* 52:633-42

McQuaig, L. 1991. *The Quick and the Dead: Brian Mulroney, Big Business and the Seduction of Canada*. Toronto: Viking Press

Magnusson, W., W.K. Carroll, C. Doyle, M. Langer, and R.B.J. Walker, eds. 1984. *The New Reality*. Vancouver: New Star Books

Magnusson, W. and R. Walker. 1988. De-Centring the State: Political Theory and Canadian Political Economy. *Studies in Political Economy* 26 (Summer):37-71

Maier, Charles S. 1987. *Changing Boundaries of the Political: Essays on the Evolving Balance between the State and Society, Public and Private in Europe*. New York: Cambridge University Press

Manser, Gordon. 1972. Implications of Purchase-of-Services for Voluntary Agencies. *Social Casework* 53 (6):335-41

Marchak, P. 1984. The New Economic Reality: Substance and Rhetoric. In *The New Reality*, edited by W. Magnusson, N.K. Carroll, C. Doyle, M. Langer, and R.B.J. Walker. Vancouver: New Star Books

Marsh, L.C. 1950. The Welfare State: Is it a Threat to Canada? In *Proceedings of the Canadian Conference on Social Work*, 30-44. Ottawa: Canadian Conference on Social Work

Mathers, D.L. 1979. Public Welfare Vancouver Style, 1910-1920. *Journal of Canadian Studies* 14 (Spring):3-10

Matthews, Carol. 1978. Buying Out: Government Funding of the Third Sector. *Social Work Perspective* 12 (Fall):3-12

Miller, S.M. 1978. The Recapitalisation of Capital. *Social Policy* (Nov.-Dec):5-12

Mishra, R. 1977. *Society and Social Policy*. London: Macmillan

– 1981. *Social Policy and Society*. London: Macmillan

– 1984. *The Welfare State in Crisis*. Brighton: Wheatsheaf Books

– 1989. Riding the New Wave: Social Work and the Neoconservative Challenge. *International Social Work* 32 (3):171-82

Morris, R. 1982. Government and Voluntary Agency Relationships. *Social Service Review* 56, 3 (Sept.):333-45

Moscovitch, A. 1986. The Welfare State since 1975. *Journal of Canadian Studies* 21:77-94

Murray, G.J. 1969. *Voluntary Organisations and Social Welfare*. Glasgow: Olive and Boyd

Musselwhite, J.C., R.B. Katz, and L.M. Salamon. 1985. *Government Spending and the Nonprofit Sector in Pittsburgh/Allegheny County*. Washington, DC: Urban Institute Press

Myles, John. 1988. Decline or Impasse? The Current State of the Welfare State. *Studies in Political Economy* 26 (Summer):73-107

– 1989. Understanding Canada: Comparative Political Economy Perspectives. *Canadian Review of Sociology and Anthropology* 26 (1):1-9

Ng, Roxana. 1988. *The Politics of Community Services: Immigrant Women, Class and State*. Toronto: Garamond Press

Ng, R., G. Walker, and J. Mueller, eds. 1990. *Community Organization and the Canadian State*. Toronto: Garamond Press

Nielsen, W.A. 1979. *The Endangered Sector*. New York: Columbia University Press

O'Connor, J.R. 1973. *The Fiscal Crisis of the State*. New York: St. Martin's Press

O'Connor, Julia. 1989. Welfare Expenditure and Policy Orientation in Canada in Comparative Perspective. *Canadian Review of Sociology and Anthropology* 26 (1):127-50

Offe, C. 1984. *Contradictions of the Welfare State*. London: Hutchinson

Olson, M. 1993. *Family Support Services*. Victoria: Ministry of Social Services Family Support Project. Mimeo

Opit, L.J. 1977. Domiciliary Care for the Elderly Sick – Economy or Neglect. *British Medical Journal* 1 (Jan.):30-3

Ostrander, S.A. 1985. Voluntary Social Service Agencies in the U.S. *Social Service Review* (Sept.):435-54

Ott, Fred. 1985. 1981-1985: What Has It Meant to the Social Services of Kelowna, B.C.? Mimeo

Palmer, J.L. and I.V. Sawhill, eds. 1982. *The Reagan Experiment*. Washington, DC: Urban Institute

People's Public Commission on Social and Community Service Cutbacks. 1982. Interim Report. Mimeo

Perlmutter, Felice. 1971. Public Funds and Private Agencies. *Child Welfare* 50:264-70

Perryman, Gavin. 1984. Privatization: What Does It Mean? Vancouver: Social Planning and Research Council of BC. Mimeo

Pfeffer, J. and Salancik, G.R. 1978. *The External Control of Organizations*. New York: Harper and Row

Pitsula, James and Ken Rasmussen. 1990. *Privatizing a Province: The New Right in Saskatchewan*. Vancouver: New Star Books

Powell, W.W. 1986. *The Nonprofit Sector: A Research Handbook*. New Haven: Yale University Press

Quebec Commission of Inquiry on Health and Social Welfare. 1976. *Report of the Commission of Inquiry on Health and Social Welfare*. (The Castonguay-Nepveu Report). Quebec City: Official Publisher

Rawls, J. 1972. *A Theory of Justice*. Oxford: Clarendon Press

Redish, A. 1984. *Is There a Social Policy in B.C.? Who Has Been Hurt and Why*. Vancouver: BC Economic Policy Institute, University of British Columbia

– 1985. *An Analysis of the 1985/86 B.C. Budget: Jousting at Windmills*. Vancouver: BC Economic Policy Institute, University of British Columbia

Rein, M., G. Esping-Andersen, and L. Rainwater, ed. 1990. *Stagnation and Renewal in Social Policy Regimes*. Armonk, NY: M.E. Sharpe

Rekart, J. 1988. *A Preliminary Study of the Impacts of Economic Changes and Shifts in Government Policy on Nonprofit Agencies Providing Family and Children's Services in British Columbia*. Vancouver: Social Planning and Research Council of BC

Rice, D. 1984. *Analysis of 1984/85 B.C. Budget*. Burnaby, BC: BC Federation of Labour

Rice, R.M. 1975. Impact of Government Contracts on Voluntary Social Service Agencies. *Social Casework* 56 (7):387-95

Robinson, D.Z. 1971. Government Contracting for Academic Research: Accountability in the American Experience. In *The Dilemma of Accountability in Modern Government: Independence versus Control*, edited by B.L.R. Smith and D.C. Hague, 103-17. New York: St. Martin's Press

Rosenbluth, G. and W. Schworm. 1984. *The New Priorities of the Social Credit Government of B.C.* Vancouver: BC Economic Policy Institute, University of British Columbia

Ross, G. and J. Jenson. 1985. Pluralism and the Decline of Left Hegemony: The French Left in Power. *Politics and Society* 14 (2):147-83

Salamon, L.M. 1987a. Of Market Failure, Voluntary Failure, and Third Party Government: Toward a Theory of Government-Nonprofit Relations in the Modern Welfare State. *Journal of Voluntary Action Research* 16 (1 & 2):29-49

- 1987b. Partners in Public Service: The Scope and Theory of Government-Nonprofit Relations. In *The Nonprofit Sector: A Research Handbook*, edited by Walter W. Powell, 99-117. New Haven: Yale University Press

- 1989. The Changing Partnership between the Voluntary Sector and the Welfare State. In *The Future of the Nonprofit Sector*, edited by V.A. Hodgkinson, R.W. Lyman, and Associates, 41-60. San Francisco: Jossey-Bass

Salamon, L.M. and A.J. Abramson. 1982. The Nonprofit Sector. In *The Reagan Experiment*, edited by J.L. Palmer and I.V. Sawhill, 219-43. Washington, DC: Urban Institute

Savas, E.S. 1981. *Privatizing the Public Sector*. Chatham, NJ: Chatham House

Schechter, S. 1982. *Women and Male Violence: The Visions and Struggles of the Battered Women's Movement*. Boston: South End Press

Schorr, Alvin. 1970. The Tasks for Voluntarism in the Next Decade. *Child Welfare* 49 (Oct.):425-34

Schumacher, E.F. 1973. *Small is Beautiful*. New York: Harper and Row

Schworm, W. 1984. *The Economic Impact of the B.C. 'Restraint' Budget*. Vancouver: BC Economic Policy Institute, University of British Columbia

Scofield, J. 1984. Recovery through Restraint? The Budgets of 1983/84 and 1984/85. In *The New Reality*, eds. W. Magnusson, W.K. Carroll, C. Doyle, M. Langer, and R.B.J. Walker, 41-5. Vancouver: New Star Books

Seebohm, R. 1968. *Report of the Committee on Local Authority and Allied Social Services*. London: HMSO

Shragge, E. 1990. Community Based Practice: Political Alternatives or New State Forms. In *Bureaucracy and Community*, edited by L. Davies and E. Shragge, 134-78. Montreal: Black Rose Books

Silver, J. and J. Hall. 1990. *The Political Economy of Manitoba*. University of Regina: Canadian Plains Research Center

Smith, B.C. 1985. *Decentralization: The Territorial Dimension of the State*. London: George Allen and Unwin

Smith, B.L.R. 1971. Accountability and Independence in the Contract State. In *The Dilemma of Accountability in Modern Government: Independence versus Control*, edited by B.L.R. Smith and D.C. Hague, 3-69. New York: St Martin's Press

- 1983. Changing Public-Private Sector Relations: A Look at the U.S. *The Annals of the American Academy* 466 (Mar.): 194-264

Smith, B.L.R. and D.C. Hague, eds. 1971. *The Dilemma of Accountability in Modern Government: Independence versus Control*. New York: St. Martin's Press

Smith, S.R. 1989. The Changing Politics of Child Welfare Services: New Roles for Government and the Nonprofit Sector. *Child Welfare* 68 (May-June):289-99

Social Planning Council of Metropolitan Toronto. 1984. Human Services for Profit: Issues and Trends. *Social Infopac* 3 (Dec.):1-6

Starr, P. 1989. The Meaning of Privatization. In *Privatization and the Welfare State*, edited by S.B. Kamerman and A.J. Kahn, 15-48. Princeton, NJ: Princeton University Press

Sugden, R. 1984. Voluntary Organisations and the Welfare State. In *Privatization and the Welfare State*, edited by J. LeGrand and R. Robinson, 70-89. London: Allen and Unwin

Swankey, B. 1985. *The Tory Budget and the Corporate Plan to Restructure Canada and How the System Really Works*. Vancouver: Centre for Socialist Education

Tappen, D. 1982. *Coping with Cutbacks*. New York: Community Council of Greater New York

Terrell, P. 1979. Private Alternatives to Public Human Services Administration. *Social Services Review* 53 (Mar.):56-74

Terrell, P. and R.M. Kramer 1984. Contracting with Nonprofits. *Public Welfare* 42, 1 (Winter):33-44

Thane, P. 1982. *The Foundation of the Welfare State*. Harlow: Longman

Thatcher, M. 1977. *Let Our Children Grow Tall*. London: Centre for Policy Studies

Therborn, G. 1984. The Prospects of Labour and the Transformation of Advanced Capitalism. *New Left Review* 145 (May/June):29-33

Titmuss, R.M. 1963. *Essays on the Welfare State*. London: Allen and Unwin

– 1968. *Commitment to Welfare*. London: Allen and Unwin

– 1970. *The Gift Relationship: From Human Blood to Social Policy*. London: Allen and Unwin

Townsend, P. and N. Davidson. 1984. *Inequalities in Health: The Black Report*. Harmondsworth: Penguin

Tucker, D.J. 1984. *An Ecological Analysis of Voluntary Social Service Organizations: Their Birth, Growth and Death*. Hamilton, ON: McMaster University

Turem, J.S. and C.E. Born. 1983. Doing More with Less. *Social Work* (May-June):206-10

Unell, J. 1979. *Voluntary Social Services: Financial Resources*. London: Bedford Square Press

United Way of the Bay Area. 1982. *Understanding Public Funding Cutbacks on Human Services: An Examination of Emerging Trends in Human Service Funding and Policy up to April, 1982, and the Impact of These Trends on the Human Service Delivery Systems in California and the San Francisco Bay Area*. San Francisco: United Way of the Bay Area

United Way of Santa Clara County, Planning and Allocations Division. 1982. *Retrenchment and Transition: An Analysis of the Impacts of Public Sector Funding Reductions on Human Services, Education and the Arts in Santa Clara County*. [San Jose]: United Way of Santa Clara County

Urban Institute. 1981. *The Economic Recovery Program and the Non-Profit Sector*. Washington, DC: Urban Institute

U.S. Small Business Administration. 1984. *Unfair Competition by Nonprofit Organizations with Small Business: An Issue for the 1980s*. Washington, DC: U.S. Small Business Administration

Vancouver School Board. 1986. *Four Years of Restraint: Four Years to Recover*. Vancouver: Vancouver School Board

Van Loon, R. 1979. Reforming Welfare in Canada. *Public Policy* 27 (Fall):469-504

Walker, A. 1982. *Public Expenditure and Social Policy*. London: Heinemann Books

– 1984a. The Political Economy of Privatisation. In *Privatisation and the Welfare State*, edited by J. LeGrand and R. Robinson, 19-44. London: Allen and Unwin

– ed. 1984b. *Social Planning: A Strategy for Socialist Welfare*. Oxford: Blackwell

Webb, A. 1979. Voluntary Social Action: In Search of a Policy. *Journal of Voluntary Action Research* 18, 1-2 (Jan/Jun):8-16

– 1981. *Collective Action and Welfare Pluralism*. London: Association of Researchers in Voluntary Action and Community Involvement

Webb, A. and Wistow, G. 1982. *Whither State Welfare? Policy and Implementation in the Personal Social Services*. London: Royal Institute of Public Administration

Webb, Sidney and Beatrice Webb. 1912. *The Prevention of Destitution*. London: Longmans

Weddell, K. 1986. Privatizing Social Services in the U.S.A. *Social Policy and Administration* 20, 1 (Mar.):14-27

Wedel, Kenneth R. 1976. Government Contracting for Purchase of Service. *Social Work* 21:101-5

Weisbrod, B.A. 1977. *The Voluntary Non-Profit Sector*. Lexington, MA: Lexington Books

– 1989. The Complexities of Income Generation for Nonprofits. In *The Future of the Nonprofit Sector*, edited by V.A. Hodgkinson, R.W. Lyman, and Associates, 103-22. San Francisco: Jossey-Bass

Wharf, B. and Marilyn Callaghan. 1982. Public Policy is a Voluntary Affair. *BC Studies* 55 (Autumn):79-93

Wilding, P. and V. George. 1984. *The Impact of Social Policy*. London: Routledge and Kegan Paul

Wilson, Deirdre. 1986. *A Profile of the Non-Profit Sector in Greater Victoria*. Victoria: Community Council of Greater Victoria and Theatre BC

Wolf, J. 1983. Changing the Social Contract: Can Voluntary Non-Profits Survive Privatization. Winnipeg: Continuing Education Division, The University of Manitoba. Mimeo

Wolfe, David. 1989. The Canadian State in Comparative Perspective. *Canadian Review of Sociology and Anthropology* 26 (1):91-125

Wolfenden Committee. 1978. *The Future of Voluntary Organisations*. London: Croom Helm

Index